Epping Forest 20 (Napier Arms)	**19** Water-works, Forest Road

For conditions see back

---

19 Water-works, Forest Road	**Epping Forest 20** (Napier Arms)

19 Water-works, Forest Road	**Epping Forest 20** (Napier Arms)

ditions see back

Nw

(151 A) London Passenger Transport Board (Trolleybuses)

623 625 685	1½d

Change at Bell Junction

Bakers Arms or Chingford Mt.	**B**illet Road or Hoe Street Stn (L.N.E.R.)

Change at Standard Junction

Bell Junction	**S**t. James Street Stn (L.N.E.R.) or Gloucester Road

Ferry Boat, Ferry Ln or Palmerston Rd	**Q**ueens Road

14 Ferry Boat Ferry Lane	Gloucester Road **16**
15 Standard Junction	Standard Junction **15**
16 Palmerston Road	Queens Road **13**
17 Bell Junction	Lea Bridge Road **12** (Markhouse Rd)
18 Wood Street	
19 Water-works, Forest Road	Epping Forest **20** (Napier Arms)

For conditions see back

Ow

(151 A) London Passenger Transport Board (Trolleybuses)

623 625 685	1½d

Change at Bell Junction

Bakers Arms or Chingford Mt.	**B**illet Road or Hoe Street Stn (L.N.E.R.)

Change at Standard Junction

Bell Junction	**S**t. James Street Stn (L.N.E.R.) or Gloucester Road

Ferry Boat, Ferry Ln or Palmerston Rd	**Q**ueens Road

14 Ferry Boat Ferry Lane	Gloucester Road **16**
15 Standard Junction	Standard Junction **15**
16 Palmerston Road	Queens Road **13**
17 Bell Junction	Lea Bridge Road **12** (Markhouse Rd)
18 Wood Street	
19 Water-works, Forest Road	Epping Forest **20** (Napier Arms)

For conditions see back

Right partial column:

Passenger Transport Board (Trolleybuses)

623 625 685	1

Change at Standard Junct

Bell Junction	**S**t. James Street Stn (L.N.E.R.) or Gloucester Road

Ferry Boat, Ferry Ln or Palmerston Rd	**Q**

14 Ferry Boat Ferry Lane	Gloucester Road
15 Standard Junction	Standard Junction
16 Palmerston Road	Queens Road
17 Bell Junction	Lea Bridge Road (Markhou
18 Wood Street	
19 Water-works, Forest Road	Epping Forest (Napier

For conditions see ba

Fz

16 J	London Transport Tramways

23 Abbey Wood	Embankment **1**
22 Basildon Road	Waterloo Bridge **2**

Gz

16 J	London Transport Tramways

23 Abbey Wood	Ser.	Embankment **1**
22 Basildon Road		Waterloo Bridge **2**

Hz

16 J	London Transport Tramways

23 Abbey Wood	Ser.	Embankment
22 Basildon Road		Wat

For B-Belle, Pork Pie and FoxyLoxy

ENGLISH ALLSORTS

FURTHER EXPLORATIONS
IN UNMITIGATED ENGLAND

Peter Ashley

Adelphi

This edition
© Adelphi Publishers 2015
Text © Peter Ashley 2015
Images © Peter Ashley
unless otherwise stated

First published in 2015
by Adelphi Publishers
50 Albemarle Street
London W1S 4BD

Text by Peter Ashley
Design by Peter Ashley
Made ready for print by
Richard Gregory
Edited by Cecily Maude

ISBN 978 0 9562387 4 0

Printed and bound in
Italy by Conti Tipocolor
Florence

Sales information
Penguin Random House
Tel: 0207 840 8463

Orders to:
Grantham Book Services
Tel: 01476 541 000

10 9 8 7 6 5 4 3 2 1

Frontispiece
Dinky Toys No. 157
Jaguar XK120 Coupé
and Coronation Oxo
tin, 1953

Endpapers
Uncut London Transport
trolleybus and tram tickets,
1937

CONTENTS

PREFACE

Open this book with reverence. It is a hymn to England – the old England, the England of beach huts and Constable skies, Fox's Glacier Mints and seed packets, which isn't a Proustian fossick through forgotten memories, because this bonfire-smelling, Labrador-by-the-fire place has never gone away. We're offered the bibliographical equivalent of a village fete, or a country house where the rooms have silted up with old tennis impedimenta, wellington boots, ancestral portraits, children's toys and zoological specimens – collections which, like this book, can't be assembled overnight, but accrete and mature over decades. There's the flavour of Marmite about it, or Gentleman's Relish; except that those are acquired tastes, which some people never do acquire. There is nothing that isn't delicious about *English Allsorts*.

We have here a scrapbook of visual impressions and written aperçus, a form that is perfect for the subject: individual, personal, intimate – qualities that are as much a part of our mostly small-scale, rapidly changing landscape as they are of the supposed eccentricity for which the English are famous.

It's undeniable that to readers of a certain age, the offering is strongly – and delectably – laced with nostalgia. Green Line buses! When did I last think of them? Not since having recourse to one when visiting a girlfriend's house in the south London suburbs – what an eternity those vehicles took. The design aesthetic, established in the 1930s, had not changed much by the 1960s, and nor had the buses themselves. There's a whole chapter on characterful cars, a celebration of the golden age of British motoring, when the M1 was still as shown in the early editions of Pevsner's Buildings of England: a concrete ribbon that is being slowly traversed by, as it might be, a Riley RM. Cars were more characterful then…with a tendency to break down in characterful ways. Oh the innocence – and individuality – we have lost. The Northamptonshire company of Weetabix is now owned by the Chinese. Globalisation has worn the globe smooth.

But nostalgia isn't the point of this book. The Englishness that the author has brought to the page is unextinguishable. You don't have to look far to find it. It's in the store cupboard, on Lyle's Golden Syrup tins (as much a design classic, for these Isles, as the Coca-Cola bottle), in the village signposts that have been overgrown by cow parsley, and in the varied building materials of market towns, above which flutters the Union Jack. Despite the efforts of the rule-makers to impose a universal order of dullness on the modern world, England still manages to do things in its own way. You only have to open the door of a garden potting shed to find out. Or to stride, with the wind in your hair, along the chalk cliffs of the south coast. Or to go into a country church. Or up the Blackpool Tower. Half the time we seem to have forgotten how special this country is through losing the eyes to see. We're become too busy to linger at beauty spots. But they're still there. Thank you, thank you, Peter Ashley, for reminding us.

And for being our companion on this journey through the enchantment, full of stories told at just the right length (which is short). One of the pleasures of this book is that, along the way, we get to know the author. This is a portrait of England, and a portrait of a man; they're as rewarding as each other, both an unmitigated delight.

Clive Aslet
August 2015

INTRODUCTION

There is a thought that Henry James (1843-1916) used the phrase 'unmitigated England' to describe thatched roofs. And in a way he did, because the phrase is actually used about Warwickshire in his *English Hours* (1905). I first read it as the opening line of John Betjeman's poem 'Great Central Railway Sheffield Victoria to Banbury' where he acknowledged the phrase by putting it in quotation marks: *'Unmitigated England'/ Came swinging down the line / That day the February sun / Did crisp and crystal shine.*

So *Unmitigated England* became the title of the first book in this trilogy that collected together photographs, scrapbook items and ephemera that I'd amassed over years of simply looking at England and wanting to record and preserve them for some kind of posterity. Having been a designer and photographer ever since I could hold a pencil properly and successfully put a film into a camera I have been fascinated by how things look. And as I grew older I realised that an awful lot of the things I saw on an everyday basis were changing, not necessarily for the

better. For instance, everybody brought up in post-war Britain, as I was, recognises that the GPO telephone box, designed by Sir Giles Gilbert Scott and approved in 1935 by a Royal Fine Art Commission, can't be bettered in design terms. But it wasn't nostalgia that made me weep for their loss, it was the abysmal standards applied to those that followed. Off-the-shelf hideous booths no better than draughty bus shelters. (Of course none of this appears to matter anymore because we're all judged to be running about taking 'selfies' on our mobile phones.)

I feared that one day we would wake up to find all our post boxes painted beige and owned by the Dutch, traditional signposts with metal letters and regular maintenance replaced everywhere by flimsy posts with peeling plastic names. (They've just put one up in our village and forgotten to put any miles on it.) All vans would be white and have crass misspelled computer lettering on their sides; anything old must be called 'retro' or 'vintage' and if not made to look like the real thing by being distressed. In China.

Could there be a more
quintessential image to
describe Unmitigated
England? Obviously
there's no guessing as
to where it was taken,
but the truly remarkable
thing is that it's 1928.

Clifton R. Adams was
commissioned by the
National Geographic
Magazine to record
farms, towns, cities
and their people. The
process is Autochrome,
introduced by the
Lumière Brothers in
1907 and involved
coating glass plates
with tiny grains of
dyed potato starch.

above

Have chocolate bars got smaller, or is it just that we've grown bigger? A sixpenny Fry's Crunch was big enough in 1956

It is of course all too easy to rant, like the old boy in the corner of the pub who tells anyone who'll listen 'It weren't like that in my day'. No it isn't, because we wouldn't want to be threatened by tuberculosis every five minutes and prefer our lavatories to be inside the house. And in many ways since the first volume some things I worried about have actually turned out OK, re-enforcing the original subtitle 'A Country Lost and Found'. I bemoaned the fact that railway station termini were disguised as shopping malls where trains just happened to arrive and depart behind the franchises, and having just let off steam they go and make a superb job of doing just that at the new St Pancras International. The original cellars where the cast iron columns were spaced to take Burton beer barrels were opened up to create a space worthy of a day out in its own right. Except for 'The Booking Office Bar' who'll take over thirteen quid off you for a fishfinger sandwich.

I also talked about 'England on Film', banging on about John Schlesinger's *Far from the Madding Crowd* (1967) and *Witchfinder General* (1968), finding now that a very creditable remake of the Hardy classic (if somewhat briefer) has been made and the witchfinder has influenced Ben Wheatley's mind-bending *A Field in England* (2013). English churches though are still taking a bashing, losing congregations as fast as the lead off the roof, and we lose more and more of very peculiarly English pubs. Those that still try to emulate the rough 'n' ready drinking parlours of the past end up being ghastly pastiches at best. Classic brands still suffer at the hands of jargon-ridden marketing managers ('we're on a journey, going forward'), but there are enough good things still out there to trigger memories with, as Jonathan Meades wrote in his preface to *More From Unmitigated England* 'synaesthesiac ease'. This volume told of Christmas Pasts, breweries, cricket

and wooden type. These timber alphabets I'd thought long forgotten, but now they're being re-discovered, as are all forms of hand-drawn lettering. Just take a look at the work of Tom Frost or Jonny Hannah.

So what's new? *English Allsorts* will be more of the same, but different. Areas of Unmitigated England hitherto unmapped will be explored. A bit like Norfolk in the fifteenth century, but a lot more personal. I couldn't do a book in this series without opening up the pantry door, so some more familiar faces will be stared at, and looking at churches will take us amidst remoter congregations, both still singing and eerily silent. My passion and ignorance for flowers and other forms of unthreatening nature (poultry excepted) are exposed, as is how graphic design was before the mouse and terrabyte. London Transport will take us for a ride through town and country, and England will be drained of colour.

LOOKING AT ENGLAND

LONDON & NORTH EASTERN RAILWAY

right
A typical resident of
Unmitigated England,
Tom Harris races a
1954 Jaguar Mk VII,
and is seen here
trying on appropriate
head gear

opposite
Cut-out sign for
Geoff Laurens'
antiques shop,
Whitstable, Kent.
Originally used
outside a restaurant
as a menu holder

There's more, but I'm very aware of taking
up your time when you could be getting on
with it. The essence of this book is simple.
I look at things, and those I like I want to
share. Be it a 1927 billhead for a turpentine
dealer, a girl leaning on a Rolls-Royce
behind a rectory, a galvanised watering
can, Len Deighton book jackets, Brighton
rock, Fakenham cauliflowers or Chalk Farm
pomegranates, they're all in here somewhere.
I hope you have as good a time sifting
through the pages as I've had putting them
together. *English Allsorts*. It's all sorts of
things about England.

NAVES & CHANCELS

CHURCHES OF ENGLAND

Three times on a Sunday I had to go to church. Except it was a red brick chapel on a crossroads in Leicester; Baptist by denomination, evangelical by inclination. A morning service, Sunday School in the afternoon and another service in the evening. Accomplished by us having to make an eight mile round trip by bus, sometimes walking, sometimes cycling when I was older.

The evening services got very trying with fire and brimstone sermons, the mornings only made bearable by the fact that my very pretty first girlfriend sat in the opposite gallery trying to avoid my adolescent tics. And then, all of a sudden, our family jumped ship *en masse* and joined the Church of England. Something to do with our minister and his ministering a little too fervently to some fallen angels and my dad being a church elder who found it all a bit too much. My eldest brother had already defected to a Victorian church in the city, and here we joined him and made our new spiritual home. I even joined the choir.

The Anglican church suited me like a snug fitting cassock, and the actual buildings became even more embued with meaning. Even as a ten year old I'd cycled from my home out into the countryside to a little church that sat alone amongst the trees opposite a Hall where you had to get the key, and I'd just sit in a pew watching the trees moving silently through the plain glass. And going behind the organ where you could lift out the smaller pipes and blow down them to great effect.

I learnt more about them from Shell Guides and Pevsner's, so now I have Ordnance maps with rings around ruined Norfolk churches; I indulge myself in the uplifting atmospheres of the superb churches out on the Romney Marsh and get very excited when I see a pristinely painted corrugated iron 'tin tabernacle'. Alone in woods, out in the fields, at the centre of village life, all hold me with their very tangible sense of the past and the continuing hope they give for the future.

NORFOLK RUINS

They could be stark jackdaw-haunted ruins on top of pre-Christian mounds; hidden in dark woods; completely covered in ivy; or covered in ivy *and* hidden in a dark wood. There are probably over a hundred ruined churches in Norfolk, more than any other county, the result of the loss of the actual villages that once surrounded them, although many were because they served what is known as 'dispersed settlement patterns'. That is not tightly-grouped cottages with the church at its nucleus, but homes and farms well spread out along the borders of pastures and greens. So the local congregations probably walked across fields much as we do, to stand in naves on reed-covered flagstones to watch slack-jawed at the unfathomable rituals being performed up in the chancel.

The gaunt ruin of St James, Bawsey, can be seen across the fields from the main road coursing its way up from Kings Lynn to Hunstanton; to reach it one has to find the track that winds its way up from Church Farm. There was a village here, destroyed by an unscrupulous landowner who preferred sheep to villagers in their cottages, typical in the 16th century. Built in the 1130s, the main body of the church is early Norman. Baptisms and burials continued in these lonely acres up until the 1770s.

Some churches were lost altogether, cliff-top positions being particularly vulnerable. The postcard opposite shows a classic Norfolk round tower at Sidestrand, east of Cromer, all that was remaining of the original St Michael's church when Clement Scott wrote his Daily Telegraph column in December 1883 to extol the virtues of 'Poppy-Land'. It is now in the sea. This rural idyll around Cromer became swamped by holidaymakers, thanks to Scott's collected writings in 1886 and the extra publicity given it by the Great Eastern Railway Company.

above
St James, Bawsey, detail

top
St James, Bawsey, from the south east

In aimless fashion I strolled on, and attracted by a ruined church tower, took a cut through the cornfields towards a cluster of farms and a distant village

From 'Poppy-Land' by
Clement Scott
(1886)

40965. CROMER.   GARDEN OF SLEEP.

On the grass of the cliff, at the edge of the steep,
God planted a garden—a garden of sleep !
'Neath the blue of the sky, in the green of the corn,
It is there that the regal red poppies are born !
Brief days of desire, and long dreams of delight,
They are mine when my poppy land cometh in sight.
Oh ! heart of my heart ! where the poppies are born,
I am waiting for thee, in the hush of the corn.

In my garden of sleep, where red poppies are spread,
I wait for the living, alone with the dead !
For a tower in ruins stands guard o'er the deep,
At whose feet are green graves of dear women asleep !
Did they love as I love, when they lived by the sea ?
Did they wait as I wait for the days that may be ?
O ! life of my life, on the cliffs by the sea,
By the graves in the grass, I am waiting for thee.

CLEMENT SCOTT.

above & top
St Andrew,
Bircham Tofts

left
Wall flowers,
Appleton

NORFOLK RUINS *(continued)*

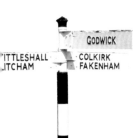

Appleton is a particular favourite, tucked away down a side road near West Newton, like Bawsey in the nexus of the Sandringham Estate. You cross a farmyard and turn right and there it is. I found it early one morning a few years back, and it was so overgrown I could hardly see any ecclesiastical outlines at all. Weeds towered over me as I waded inside, sheep looked balefully at me from the adjoining pasture where the deserted village once stood. My next visit saw that all had been very beneficially cleared away to reveal the 12th century round tower and a slab commemorating 17th century Pastons, later relatives of the letter writing family.

St Andrew in Bircham Tofts is now so overgrown with ivy it could easily be mistaken for a huge box of hedge. So sad too, to see that the churchyard is an ocean of plant life bent on engulfing the tombstones.

Godwick was a medieval village abandoned sometime in the 17th century, leaving just a large barn and hollows that tell of the lost streets. A manor house here may have hastened the end with the removal of cottages, but this too has gone. It was the home of the Coke family before they decamped to Holkham, and the present Godwick Hall was built in the 1840s.

So much good work has been done to save all Norfolk churches from the ravages of time, by both public bodies like the county council, together with stirling efforts by The Churches Conservation Trust and the Norfolk Churches Trust founded by Lady Harrod in 1976. I do hope that the simple and beautifully atmospheric church at Barmer, embowered in trees across a field near Syderstone survives, *not* as a ruin, but as the only reminder now of the name.

KNOWLTON

The first time I saw Knowlton church in east Dorset a group of people were standing in the surrounding earthwork in a circle, watching others in top hats miming a burial. What that was about I failed to stop and ask and drove on into the winter's gloom to Cranborne. The next time I came it was high summer and the embankment was host to many wild flowers. Around in the fields are the remains of Neolithic henges and Bronze Age barrows, mostly now ploughed out. The church itself, with its 12th century chancel and 14th century tower, was the parish church for the deserted village, falling into ruin in the 18th century. But it is still a useful reminder that the Christian religion made use of ancient sites, putting their church in the centre of the earthwork both as an indicator of a new code and perhaps also as an altruistic gesture towards the adherents to older beliefs.

That there is a feeling of ancient past rituals here is unmistakeable. Much can be conjectured about the pair of yew trees that would once have had great significance here. Almost certainly they pre-date the church, and are in constant use as an evergreen repository for votive offerings. I was beset with the notion that they were twin guardians of something extremely old, and as such shouldn't be interfered with. Shades of M.R. James' ghost stories and warnings to the far too curious.

RECULVER

James Bond drove down this way in Ian Fleming's *Goldfinger* (1959): 'He came up with a crossroads. To the left the signpost said RECULVER. Underneath was the ancient monument sign for Reculver church. Bond slowed, but didn't stop'.

You see the twin towers across the fields as you approach this outpost on the Kent coast, a little to the east of Herne Bay. They are all that is substantially left of St Mary's Abbey, originally built in the middle of a decayed Roman fort around AD 670. The local vicar pulled down most of it in 1809 for the curious reason that it was feared it would become a 'peepshow'. But after the timely intervention of Trinity House, who quickly

recognised their value as a seamark, the towers were left perched on the cliff edge.

Reculver, or Regulbium, was a Roman *castrum* built to guard the northern end of the Wantsum channel, the southern end being at Richborough and effectively turning this eastern end of Kent into the Isle of Thanet. Parts of the wall can still be seen in the undergrowth to the east of the towers, and indeed a close inspection of the ruined abbey walls reveals flat Roman tiles amongst the flint and rubblestone.

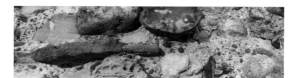

St Mary, Kenardington, Kent

St Andrew, Limpsfield Chart, Surrey

St Andrew, Little Snoring, Norfolk

St Denis, Aswarby, Lincolnshire

Southease, East Sussex

St Andrew, Tur Langton, Leicestershire

Peter & St Paul, Ash, Kent

St Peter & St Paul, Belton, Lincolnshire

Andrew, Beddingham, East Sussex

All Saints, Barmer, Norfolk

Andrew, Welham, Leicestershire

St Nicholas, Thistleton, Rutland

ROMNEY MARSH

above
King Penguin
Romney Marsh
(1950)

above right
The barn-like
St Mary's at
East Guldeford,
East Sussex

top
Text board,
St Dunstan's
Snargate, Kent

Draw a line between Hythe in Kent and Rye in Sussex and the triangular wedge of land pointing down to the south east is the Romney Marsh. In fact this is the generic name for the Walland, Denge and Guldeford Marshes, and the pointed tip is the shifting shingle of Dungeness. To the north west the line of low hills is the old coastline, and everything here was once under the sea. The villages are sparse, often just a handful of farms and cottages, and their churches are equally plain and simple.

They are medieval, and remarkably have for the most part escaped the endeavours of the Victorian 'restorer'. Instead they rejoice in Georgian box pews, oval text boards and big escutcheons over altars and chancel arches where George III coats-of-arms show lions and unicorns fighting for the crown. 'The churches will please the ecclesiologist', wrote painter John Piper in his King Penguin *Romney Marsh*. They should more than please everyone; I'm continually drawn back to the Marsh, and their presence.

Piper likened St Mary in the Marsh to 'a rural Norfolk church as drawn by Cotman' and as the wind blows across from the nearby sea this is easy to imagine. I had to run inside to escape the rain that swept across the Marsh and just as quickly cleared leaving bright sunshine. The red tiled floor contains fragments of half-forgotten memorial stones and outside in the churchyard Edith Nesbit, author of *The Railway Children* and much besides, is buried. She died, probably of lung cancer, in 1924 in New Romney.

Another author, Richard Barham, who wrote *The Ingoldsby Legends*, was rector at St Dunstan's in Snargate. Which appears at first glance to be little more than the church and a remarkable 'Unmitigated' pub, The Red Lion. (No wretched piped music here. Just good beer and even better conversation.) The church has an embossed inscription on a lead plate, a puzzling glimpse of workmen in the 18th century: 'J. Bourne, C. Warden-Warrington plumber T. Apps carpenter and all his jolly men, 1780'.

ROMNEY MARSH (continued)

Brookland is one of the larger Marsh villages, and probably because of unstable soil St Augustine's church has a detached campanile. Standing aloof to one side of the porch it is quirkily described by Sheila Kaye-Smith in her novel *Joanna Godden*: '…a peculiar and unexplained erection, shaped like a pagoda, in three tiers of black and battered tar-boarding. [It] suggested nothing so much as a disreputable Victorian widow in tippet, mantle and crinoline, seeking the support of a stone wall after a carouse'. Kaye-Smith called the village 'Brodnyx' and as enjoyable as her book is the film made of it in 1947: *The Loves of Joanna Godden* with music by Vaughan Williams and a liberty-taking screenplay by H.E. Bates.

The film features shots of St Clement's in Old Romney where now Derek Jarman is buried in the churchyard. The filmic theme continues inside. Walt Disney and Rank shot *The Scarecrow of Romney Marsh* (1963) here with Patrick McGoohan, and painted the pews ointment pink. The villagers, all three of them perhaps, voted to keep them as we see them today. The film was based on *Doctor Syn*, another essential Marsh novel by Russell Thorndike.

**above, right
& below**
St Thomas a Becket,
Fairfield, Kent

Although seen completely out of context, perhaps the images we will remember of these churches won't be John Piper's paintings but frames from films. I can't talk about St Thomas a Becket at Fairfield now without mentioning its appearance in recent years in both Mike Newell's 2012 *Great Expectations* and in the same year (perhaps they shared location catering) *Parade's End* with Benedict Cumberbatch. But all these very brief moments can't make up for seeing them in the stone and brick, as it were. To walk out over the sheep-nibbled meadows and negotiating the dykes to the very sensitively restored (W.D. Caroe 1913) St Thomas a Becket is one of the most atmospheric

things one can do in one of the most atmospheric places in England, but make sure you've got the key. The exterior walls are seemingly quite modern, and they are, a brick and tiled cloak over a timber frame that looks original. Caroe wisely left the box pews and the plain 18th century three-decker pulpit alone. Sitting in here on a late summer's evening it's easy to imagine a rector hurrying between the sheep and over the water courses in a billowing gown, his congregation a handful of farmers and their households already impatiently ensconced in their respective pews. As the last of the day's sun shines down on the stone font a verger goes round with a taper lighting the oil lamps as the first hymn is sung.

BUS STOPS & ESCALATORS
LONDON TRANSPORT

Its name is Transport for London, in the current irritating vogue for turning a simple name into a sentence or phrase. Like English Heritage calling their Festival of History 'History Live!' as if that exclamation mark would make us all go running around waving our hands in the air. So we'll stick with 'London Transport' because that's what we'll look at and it's once what was on the side of tube trains and buses alike.

If all the books that have been written about this mass transit system were laid end to end they would probably reach round the Circle Line. Well, between Notting Hill Gate and Bayswater at least. It is the reference point for so many enthusiasms. If your bag is disused Underground stations then you can not only read copious amounts about them but also be taken down into their ghostly interiors if you latch on to the right set of *Undergroundistas*. And just travelling can be compulsive when you can board a train at Farringdon and disembark an hour later in the leafy Chilterns at Amersham. Or change and be even further out in Chesham.

Taking a London bus is by far the best way to see the capital, my own taste extending to the front seat upstairs of a regular service rather than the breezy top deck of a tourist bus. With a bit of luck it may be a Routemaster that takes you by St Paul's, but whatever it is it will be in a smart red livery by Mayoral dictate. Red buses, black cabs, the colours of London.

I can think of no other organisation whose culture and heritage is so varied and interesting. From ground-breaking architecture started in the early twentieth century, which still continues today, to highly desirable posters and artefacts. This chapter will of course only skim the tactile surfaces, but I can assure you that the Museum in Covent Garden will send you on amazing journeys. The last time I was in there I couldn't help buying a scarf in the same pattern as the Routemaster bus seat moquette. You can buy a sofa made-up in it too, but that may be taking a big passion a little too far. Inviting people to sit down and then pressing a 'Push Once' bell. Twice.

LONDON BUSES

above
Routemaster bell push

above centre
Detail of RTL 1076.
Note the utilitarian
chrome spring clip
holding down the
bonnet

above right
Routemaster buses
in Oxford Street

below
Postcard of Piccadilly
Circus, Franz Lazi
1964. The London
Pavilion is showing
one of the flagship
Unmitigated England
films, *Tom Jones*

In the postcard below of Piccadilly Circus, taken in 1964 by Franz Lazi, every bus is an 'RT'. The prototype appeared just before the war, and between then and 1979 it achieved a production run of 7,000, a record still not broken for a bus produced specifically for one city. Designed jointly by London Transport and AEC, this was the forerunner of the much-loved Routemaster (RM) that although now phased-out is still in service on 'heritage' routes 9 and 15.

The classic Routemaster made its debut at the 1954 Commercial Motor Exhibition in Earl's Court. Initially it was a replacement for the defunct trolley buses, but by 1968 2,760 had been produced, and drivers, conductors and passengers all loved it.

Styled by Douglas Scott in lightweight aluminium, comfort was achieved with independent front suspension, shock absorbers and warm air heating. This was the bus (No. 94) that carried me into town from Bedford Park, Chiswick. Its open rear platform was very useful to take a running jump at if one had cut it too fine to the bus stop in South Parade.

above
Archway bound
390, another
Routemaster in
Oxford Street

**above centre
and right**
The new Routemaster
in Victoria

below
A contemporary
three-colour
photograph of an
AEC Regent
STL-Type bus,
1931

Post Routemaster we had to endure the appalling bendy buses and worse until Heatherwick Studio's new Routemaster took to the streets in 2012, manufactured in Northern Ireland by Wrightbus. The first was seen on route 38. In the London Mayoral election of 2012 Ken Livingstone vowed to scrap the whole project in favour of ones powered by either Ever Ready batteries or people on the lower deck pedalling. Odd really, considering the new vehicle is the 'greenest' red bus to be designed just for the capital. Thankfully he lost, and London's streetscape will be transformed as production of the Boris Bus (named after the mayor who promoted its service) now approaches 800. The design does everything a London bus should. I particularly like the rear curving window that lights the steps up to the top deck, somehow a nod to the folk memory of the outside staircases on horse drawn and motor buses of the early twentieth century. A girl in the driving cab of one at Victoria told me it's '...the best bus I've ever driven'.

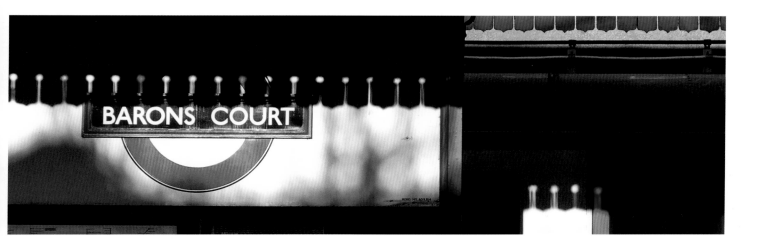

UNDERGROUND STATIONS

above
Barons Court,
Piccadilly Line
1905

opposite
Kennington,
Northern Line
1890

below
Underground *Diagram
of Lines* 1966, based
on Harry Beck's
original map

It's called the Underground, although much of this railway system is in fact out in the open air. After the tight enclosure beneath London's streets it always pleases me to leave Earls Court station on the Piccadilly Line to await the burst of light as the train clatters up into Barons Court. The frenetic rush on city platforms replaced now by the opening doors letting in the suburban breezes from South Ealing, Northfields, Boston Manor, until plunging into the Middlesex earth again to circumnavigate Heathrow Airport. Stations we don't always see much of other than as part of our hurried journeys, but all very identifiable by both the very conscious recognition of the Underground roundel and, less so perhaps, by their architecture.

As the system developed in the early twentieth century a consistent identity became crucial. What had started out as a solid red disc and blue bar between 1908 and 1915 became rationalised to the familiar red-ringed roundel in 1918 by the arts and crafts calligrapher Edward Johnston for use on both the Underground and General buses. His superb typography (now tinkered with) gave a cohesive feel to station signs and communications. His friend Eric Gill worked with him on it, leading directly to Gill's own famous sans serif typeface. Equally part of the identity became Harry Beck's 1933 much copied diagrammatic map of the system.

The buildings became as important to the corporate image as the signs. I don't think there is more innovative design on any other system. From the new 'ox blood' glazed surfaces of Leslie Green's stations to the classic 1930s rotundas by Charles Holden, London Transport gained a unique presence in the capital's streetscape.

above
Ticket office surround,
Hampstead, Northern
Line. Opened 1907

top left
Edward Bawden
illustration from
Visitor's London,
London Transport
1954

top right
Exterior, Chalk Farm,
Northern Line
Opened 1907

UNDERGROUND STATIONS *(continued)*

There was no compromise in Leslie Green's early twentieth century stations. With his assistants Stanley A. Heaps and Israel Walker he was responsible for over forty of them, and although his was a standardised pattern each one of them was adapted to a particular site. Straightforward oblongs on rectangular corners (the wireless-famous Mornington Crescent), snub-nosed features at sharply-angled road junctions (Chalk Farm), no two Green stations are alike, although they follow a flamboyant classical style made even more recognisable to passengers by an exterior surface using moulded terracotta. In turn these were glazed in a deep-red colour known in architectural terms as *sang de boeuf*, or 'ox blood'. Arched windows above ground level were a prominent feature, from a single one at Arsenal (built as Gillespie Road) to fourteen at Chalk Farm.

Before the advent of the rationalised Underground roundel, the lettering for station names, the name or initials of the original operating company and entrance signs were moulded as part of the station fabric. In addition a decorative cartouche could adorn a corner or emphasise the joining of arches. The entrance halls became terrariums of pomegranates and acanthus leaves, friezes of green tiles beneath cream or white paintwork. The ticket office openings continued the theme with curvy art nouveau surrounds.

Down on the platforms tiling continued, white or cream punctuated with coloured tiles in varying geometric patterns. Pale blue at Camden Town, dark blue at Kings Cross. This was before posters started to appear, so the station name was picked out in a contrasting coloured tile. 'Heath Street', the original name for Hampstead, can still clearly be seen.

At one time in the dark ages all these impressive monuments to the development of a capital city could have been swept away and replaced by something banal and insignificant. Fortunately we live (for the present) in enlightened times, and much of these things are now carefully preserved. Even if something past its usefulness needs replacing the chances are that an exact copy will be made. An Unmitigated afternoon can be spent hopping on and off Northern Line stations at, for example, Chalk Farm and Hampstead to take it all in. Run your finger over a pomegranate at the former, or the now obsolete 'In' and 'Out' signs at the latter that are still there just for our pleasure.

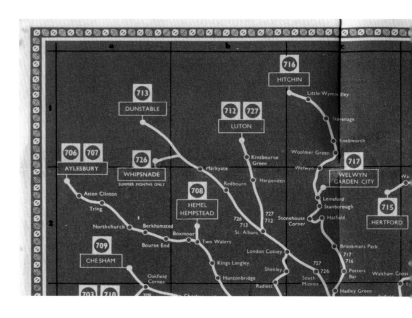

LONDON IN THE COUNTRY

In these days of little or no thought being given to bus liveries, it seems even more remarkable now that London Transport made a very conscious decision before the Second World War to have green buses on their rural routes, instead of the classic red used in the city. Green Line coaches started on three routes in July 1930, and immediately benefitted from passengers finding railway travel increasingly sooty. Initially they were single deck vehicles in a variety of guises, later the flat-fronted AEC Regal RF which stayed in service for over 20 years from its first run in 1951. After the arrival of the Routemasters the comfort required on longer journeys meant that the more economical double-deckers could now be put into service.

'We're going by Green Line' said my father as we decamped from St Pancras station and took the Underground to Baker Street, to then stand in the dark and drizzle at a bus stop. Mystified, wondering if I would ever see my great aunt in the Chilterns, I waited impatiently until out of the gloom came Green Line 709 for Chesham. Above the side windows was a long panel that said Wrotham-Victoria-Chesham.

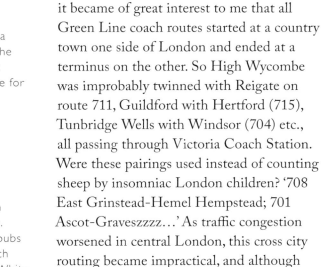

above

Detail of a 1939
Leyland TF Green
Line coach. Note a
distorted use of the
London Transport
roundel as a frame for
the radiator cap

above right

Green Line
Button Badge

right

Green Line Coach
Tickets, actual size.
A fair number of pubs
were used as coach
stops: Sevenoaks White
Hart, Hildenborough
New Cock Inn

Or maybe the other way round. Anyway, it became of great interest to me that all Green Line coach routes started at a country town one side of London and ended at a terminus on the other. So High Wycombe was improbably twinned with Reigate on route 711, Guildford with Hertford (715), Tunbridge Wells with Windsor (704) etc., all passing through Victoria Coach Station. Were these pairings used instead of counting sheep by insomniac London children? '708 East Grinstead-Hemel Hempstead; 701 Ascot-Graveszzzz…' As traffic congestion worsened in central London, this cross city routing became impractical, and although Green Line still exists its truncated route system seems to be for connecting airports with places like Legoland.

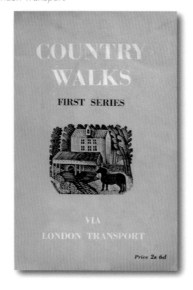

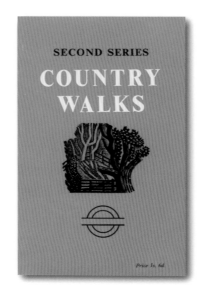

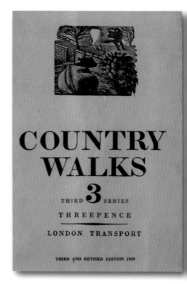

LONDON IN THE COUNTRY (continued)

More local ambitions in country travel around the Home Counties were met by green buses emblazoned 'London Transport' just like their red counterparts, later becoming 'London & Country' which seemed about right. These were the single deckers pulled up outside rural stations, the driver with a white top to his cap and a grey jacket talking to the tobacconist from the ubiquitous Finlay's. Or alongside a parade of mock half-timbered shops built after the arrival of the station.

Both Green Line and London & Country buses were used by those wanting to rid themselves of city grime and get out onto country footpaths. This was the age of the mass weekend migration that started after the First World War, people wanting to 'get back to nature'. Or even earlier: Leonard Bast in E.M. Forster's *Howard's End*:

As I came out of the office I said to myself, "I must have a walk once in a way. If I don't take this walk now, I shall never take it". I had a bit of dinner at Wimbledon, and then–.

above
Illustration from
the *Country Walks*
booklets

above right
London & Country
bus photographed
off-piste at Kingscote
Station on the Bluebell
Railway in Sussex

right
Country Buses folding
map, 1968

Ideas promoted by London Transport of course, with a wealth of posters and literature telling of the bucolic delights awaiting you as you stepped off a green bus or exited from a station. A series of *Country Walks* booklets gave precise instructions on how to get there: 'Chorley Wood by Green Line Coach Route 703 or by Metropolitan Line train from Baker Street Station', and told you what to look out for: 'Flaunden…the gardens have cob-trees, and the hedges are notable for holly.'

I asked a friend who was brought up in Stanwell, Middlesex in the 1960s what she knew of Green Lines and London & Country and she said: 'They were like magic buses, they took us to places we only knew from jigsaws and chocolate boxes'.

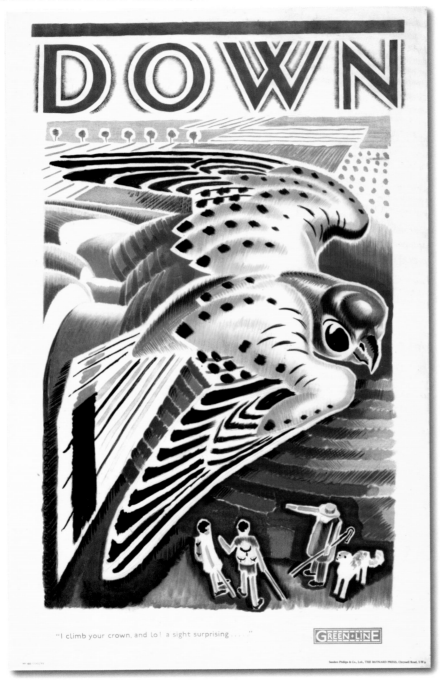

"I climb your crown, and lo! a sight surprising...."

GREEN·LINE

LONDON TRANSPORT POSTERS

Frank Pick (1878-1941), along with Jack Beddington at Shell, became one of the foremost patrons of designers and artists. In 1908 he was Publicity Manager for the London Underground and in 1912 the Commercial Officer with a remit that now included buses. In time he became Vice Chairman and Chief Executive. Early on he commissioned Edward Johnston to sort out the identity, and embarked on a programme that saw some of the finest posters ever used by a commercial organisation. There was no fixed fee (more experience, more money) and Pick kept the brief as open as possible. The aim was, of course, simple. To increase passenger traffic in literally every direction.

**above &
opposite left**

Four posters by
Clifford and
Rosemary Ellis,
1933

opposite right

For when you got
there, a walkers'
handbook, 1934

In the 1930s Charles Holden's new stations had lighting columns that included the station name and a pair of poster display boards. This meant that numerous 'pair' posters could be produced which enabled the designer to use the entire area of the left hand side for an image, leaving the right hand area to take the relevant wording. As an illustrator, Len Deighton produced his only poster for London Transport, *London's Village Life* in 1957, five years later going on to immediate success with his novel *The Ipcress File*.

It's impossible here to illustrate just how desirable all the posters are now, so I have chosen just one series, by Clifford and Rosemary Ellis. Married in 1931, it's never been entirely clear who did what in their collaborations that included work for Shell, the Empire Marketing Board and the General Post Office. Later they designed nearly a hundred book jackets for the Collins 'New Naturalist' series. Here they encouraged journeys by four departments: Down (Green Line), Heath (Underground), River (Trolleybus) and Wood (General buses). These and a great many others can be seen on the London Transport Museum's website or at the marvellous Museum itself in Covent Garden. I want a complete set of the Ellis originals on my wall.

TEA & CLOCKWORK

UNMITIGATED BRANDS

Not long ago Tate & Lyle celebrated 125 years of Lyle's Golden Syrup by subverting their own classic can with suitably celebratory phrases and advice about how to use this pantry staple. Unlike the examples opposite they also flipped the colours to produce largely golden tins. I've always loved this treacly receptacle, an ever constant presence on our 50s tea table with its engraving of a dead lion and Biblical riddle. How good was that, and even better that it has never become a victim of a marketing make-over. Until these tins appeared, of course.

So you know what happened, immediately I wanted every variant and so was seen on my hands and knees in supermarkets fishing about at the backs of shelves for elusive cans. Not just my own supermarket. It could be Morrisons in Buxton, Waitrose in Cambridge, and not just me but an army of shopping girlfriends who had to put themselves in compromising positions in order to complete my quest. And no, I didn't call them the Treacle Tarts.

Why did I do it? It's not as if I even use the stuff except for dipping a spoon in it now and then. One of the girls who makes marvellous cakes comes round now and then to decant from the collection, but I have so little room that the cans are stowed away in what could be perpetual storage. I suppose it's the familiarity of brands from childhood, and the often original and exciting ways that they were promoted. A red stereoscopic viewer from Weetabix, the foreplay between the demure lady and raffish soldier on the Quality Street tin and dear old Bertie Bassett. Even if you've got a liquorice allergy you'd be hard pushed not to like a figure made up of Allsorts running about.

I suppose the appeal comes from being a designer for much of my life, and these things are bound to get collected, or admired for the quality of tradition, like Tiptree jam labels. Even my mother saved up tokens on Force Flake packets to buy me a Sunny Jim doll as a present. And that was when I was thirty.

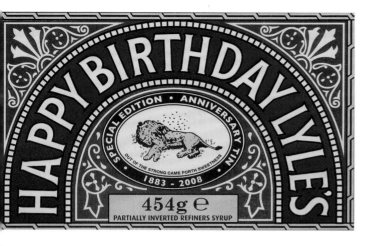

HAPPY BIRTHDAY LYLE'S

SPECIAL EDITION · ANNIVERSARY TIN
OUT OF THE STRONG CAME FORTH SWEETNESS
1883 – 2008
454g ℮
PARTIALLY INVERTED REFINERS SYRUP

FANTASTIC IN FLAPJACKS

SPECIAL EDITION · ANNIVERSARY TIN
OUT OF THE STRONG CAME FORTH SWEETNESS
1883 – 2008
454g ℮
PARTIALLY INVERTED REFINERS SYRUP

125 GOLDEN YEARS

SPECIAL EDITION · ANNIVERSARY TIN
OUT OF THE STRONG CAME FORTH SWEETNESS
1883 – 2008
454g ℮
PARTIALLY INVERTED REFINERS SYRUP

PERFECT IN PUDDINGS

SPECIAL EDITION · ANNIVERSARY TIN
OUT OF THE STRONG CAME FORTH SWEETNESS
1883 – 2008
454g ℮
PARTIALLY INVERTED REFINERS SYRUP

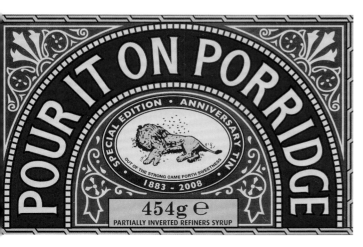

POUR IT ON PORRIDGE

SPECIAL EDITION · ANNIVERSARY TIN
OUT OF THE STRONG CAME FORTH SWEETNESS
1883 – 2008
454g ℮
PARTIALLY INVERTED REFINERS SYRUP

LYLE'S GOLDEN SYRUP

SPECIAL EDITION · ANNIVERSARY TIN
OUT OF THE STRONG CAME FORTH SWEETNESS
1883 – 2008
454g ℮
PARTIALLY INVERTED REFINERS SYRUP

WEETABIX

In the 1950s we made regular family railway excursions to Wellingborough to see my grandmother. On the return journey, usually at night, I would cup my eyes against the compartment or corridor window as the train approached Kettering, because on the right I wanted to see the big red neon sign for 'Weetabix' on their Burton Latimer factory. I knew all about Weetabix because the bright yellow box was a frequent visitor to our kitchen table, and as I munched through the neat wheaten biscuits I would study the packet in detail. For a while they had cut-out models for young 'uns to make once the contents was eaten, which meant the scissoring out of something like a cardboard copy of the latest diesel railbus and the hamfisted glueing of tab A to tab B. But by 1956 Weetabix were putting full colour stereo cards in the boxes, with an offer for a red plastic viewer for only 1/6.

In 1932 Britain saw the 'whole wheat cereal' being produced in a disused mill in Burton Latimer, the brand name 'Weetabix' following in 1936. The few traditional factory roofs I saw in the 50s are still there by the railway line, but are now dwarfed by a huge complex of blue and white buildings badged with the familiar red disc with its ear of wheat. Still part of an Unmitigated breakfast perhaps, but English? In 2012 Weetabix sold 60% of its shares to the state-owned Bright Foods in China, who also own Filippo Berio Olive Oil, such is the globalisation of famous brands. The latest Weetabix pack invites me to make a face with a biscuit and some fruit, (a 'Weetabuddy') and upload a picture of it to 'Weetabuddies.com' in order to win a 'Weetabuddy Creator Kit'. A different world; I almost yearn for the immediacy of the scissors and paste cardboard diesel railbus on a rainy morning. Well, perhaps not.

TIPTREE

Tiptree is a village to the south west of Colchester, on a road that peters out at Tollesbury on the Blackwater Estuary. And Tiptree is the name on the exquisite labels adorning the glass jam jars of Wilkin & Sons. This is how factories in Unmitigated England should be, set in the mellow countryside that provides most of its fruits, with a little museum and teashop attached. One is only surprised that the lanes aren't blocked with coaches containing thirsty WI members homing in like bees on their scones with Little Scarlet strawberry jam.

It was in 1864 that Arthur Charles Wilkin started growing strawberries, raspberries and blackcurrants. Destined for the London markets, the produce often arrived in an unsaleable condition owing to the vagaries of the railway from nearby Kelvedon to the metropolis. So Arthur turned his attention to making the fruits of the fields into jam, encouraged in 1885 by a speech by William Ewart Gladstone commending fruit growing and preserving. Arthur sent him a sample of his first jam which was met with warm prime ministerial approval.

The classic Tiptree oval label, with its royal appointment and hand-drawn script, now adorns not just jams and marmalades, but honey, (I regularly spoon in some English Borage), teas, mincemeat, Christmas Puddings. The list is long and mouth-watering, and look out too for the tall bottles of tomato ketchup and brown sauce.

TY-PHOO TEA

above
Ty-Phoo *'Trees of The Countryside'* card, inserted into packets c1936

above left to right
4 oz packets from, left to right, 1950s, 1960s and 1970s. The middle packet was the subject of three 'tea paintings' by David Hockney whilst at the Royal College of Art in the early 1960s

The Ty-Phoo Tea packet (above left) was one of a string of exotica that came out of the grocery delivery basket in my post-war England, along with the Lyle's Golden Syrup tin and my father's Player's Cigarettes. John Sumner, the son of a Coleshill grocer and tea dealer, was told by his sister that her prediliction for getting indigestion was considerably reduced when she drank small particled tea instead of the usual large leaf variety. John bought thirty chests of the tea and decided to sell it in packets as opposed to loose over the counter. Most tea at this time came from China, so he needed something oriental as a brand name. Much tea and list making later he came up with

'Ty-Phoo Tipps' and 557lbs of the tea were packed in its first year, 1903. I have also heard it said that 'Ty-Phoo' means 'doctor' in Chinese, but I would be doubtful about shouting it in an oriental emergency.

In the mid 1930s Ty-Phoo Tea had beautiful cards inside the packet, and although they reappeared later I was always disappointed that in my childhood they expected you to cut a dull monochrome picture of a footballer off the side of the box. The exotica on the packets lessened over the years, but nevertheless I liked the very plain red packet, with or without roses.

SWAN VESTAS

I never quite understood how you were supposed to light an original 'vesta', it being a wooden stick soaked in wax. Presumably you ignited one by stuffing it into the fire. Everyone must have sighed with relief when Swan Wax Matches, manufactured by Collard & Kendall in 1880s Bootle on Merseyside, became proper matches made by Bryant & May and packaged as Swan Vestas in 1906.

It was only recently that I realised that the Swan Vestas legend 'The Smoker's Match' had been dropped for some time. The thought that someone might take up smoking as a result of reading it seems slightly odd considering Swan's other branded products include cigarette papers, filter tips and lighter fuel. It's that word 'smoking' you see, but I suppose that 'The Original' is better than 'The Arsonist's Match'. Anyway, this classic English brand is now made by the Swedish Match company, along with England's Glory.

left
From top to bottom, boxes from c1930s-50s, 1970s, 1990s and 2015. Note the changing direction of the swimming swan

far left
Counter display box c1994

49

FOX'S GLACIER MINTS

There was once an advertisement painted on a gable end in Leicester that I always looked out for from the top of the bus. It fascinated me, the polar bear on top of a clear mint. Why not a fox? This debate became the basis of numerous television commercials, but back in 1922 a worker at Fox's Braunstone factory in Leicester won an in-house competition to name the mint and come up with an idea to promote it. 'Glacier Mints' and a polar bear standing on ice was his idea, and he got a fiver for it. Which even in 1922 seems horribly mean considering the ensuing success of the idea.

Fox's used a stuffed polar bear called Peppy for display at the factory, and with four others he was used at exhibitions and fairs around the country. But eventually they fell out of favour and Peppy was donated to Leicester Museums and forgotten. Until he was discovered in a store in 2003 and restored to pristine condition. It took six years, and was offered back to Fox's, now just a flagship brand in the 'portfolio' of Big Bear (big bear, geddit?). But they got all sniffy about it, calling it 'gory' as if there was blood dripping from its mouth. The firm's brand manager typically said: 'It's not the most politically correct thing to have a giant bear hanging around when they're facing extinction because of melting ice caps'. Oh dear, why don't you forget all about the nasty bear that's part of your heritage and put a fluffy-wuffy fox on the mint instead. Or send an ice cap a fiver.

above
The one ounce
packet of
Player's Digger

below
A K&P Peterson
pipe

PLAYER'S DIGGER TOBACCO

My Uncle Joe smoked Player's Digger in his pipe. In fact he was my great uncle, and I worshipped him. Even his name was right because he always reminded me of Joe Gargery in *Great Expectations*. 'Now then Pip old chap'. He lived in Lee Common in Buckinghamshire with my mum's Auntie Dora, and when we all descended on them I got worried about where we'd all sleep. 'Well, old chap' he said. 'As you're the youngest we'll put you in the bed first. Then when you're asleep we'll take you out and prop you against the wall and put the next one in.' My mouth agape he then told me that in the morning they'd do it all in reverse. Later I realised just how like H.E. Bates' Uncle Silas he was, particularly over a dummy tobacco packet. I was ten, and ran down the village street to his allotment. 'Hello old chap' he said, putting the last shreds of Digger into his pipe. The white packet was still so pristine he told me to go and fill it with soil, and he then sealed it up and told me to go and place it in the middle of the road. We watched over the hedge (I must have been standing in a wheelbarrow) as an elderly mate of Joe's made his slow progress up the street. He stopped at the packet, looked round anxiously as he pocketed it, hobbling off at almost breakneck speed as Joe and I stifled our giggles. 'How about that, chap?'

Player's introduced the brand in 1917, a tricky time internationally. A lot of Australian soldiers were in England, and their self-styled nickname of 'diggers' became even more relevant in trench warfare. It started in the gold rush days, and is a term still used in Australia today for a soldier.

QUALITY STREET

The first time I saw a tin of Quality Street I was very bemused by the Regency (or 'old-fashioned' as I thought) lady and the dashing soldier. What was she doing, offering him sweets from a big tin? In the street? I also thought he was standing a bit too close to her, but then I read *Far From The Madding Crowd* and understood about ladies and soldiers. *Quality Street* was a 1901 play written by J.M. Barrie, later adapted into two films with a couple of the characters adopted in the 1930s by Mackintosh to be Miss Sweetly and Major Quality.

It seems strange that these two folk should no longer be associated with the brand, taking their leave in 2000 from the boxes and tins. The contents appear to have changed over the years (what happened to that gorgeous strawberry wrapper?), but not the appalling habit of certain people to put their discarded wrappers back in the tin. I think there's at least just one left but no, there's only a pile of brightly-coloured cellophane and the blue coconut ones that nobody wants anyway.

BASSETT'S LIQUORICE ALLSORTS

Sometime in the late 1980s there was a lull in the studio I worked in. It was at the end of a hard week and as I watched heavy rain coursing down the windows somebody said 'I really fancy some liquorice allsorts'. A junior was dispatched across the road, and there followed the usual fight to secure the single all-liquorice Bertie Bassett figure from the box. I picked out the double-tiered black and white cube and found myself saying, 'This is new'. 'No it's not', said my mate who sat opposite me, and we had a ridiculous bet. Our secretary typed a letter to Bassett's, and I lost. But we were sent a whole big box full of just the offending allsort and we pledged to buy a box a week.

Apparently the allsorts weren't originally mixed together. In 1899 an unimpressed wholesaler in Leicester watched as 'Bassett Traveller' Charlie Thompson accidentally spilt his individual sweets over the counter where they became mixed-up together. Mr. Walker, the customer, announced that he'd buy them if they came like this. And so the Liquorice Allsort was born, and Bertie became their mascot. Later he underwent a liquorice make-over, but I think I preferred the earlier, slightly sinister manifestation, the multi-pied piper of the story book above. In those days I wonder if 'Bassett Travellers' put on a round pink coconut head before going into a shop? Probably not.

HORNBY O GAUGE

above
Hornby O Gauge
Porter

below
Post war Hornby
No. 40 Reversing
Tank Engine, Shell
Oil Tanker, Southern
Railway Milk Wagon,
Hornby Tinplate
railway station

Where once there was a scramble to release the products of Binns Road from the toy box, now there is equally frenetic activity between larger boys (and, I know, girls) on eBay for the same Dinky Toys, Hornby Trains and fiddly bits of Meccano. For us the middle years of the 20th century are lit by the auric glow of these beautifully made distractions to our school days. Whilst Dinky Toys of the 1950s held particular allure for me, it was our Hornby O Gauge clockwork trains that saw us at our most inventive.

I had inherited my much older brothers' train set: a cheapo 'M' series red locomotive and tender, a more expensive black tank engine, a handful of open trucks and enough track to go round the living room carpet. That was until the middle brother came struggling up the lane from Leicester market with a big Kellogg's box full of track. There was enough to go from the bottom of the garden by the empty pond to the front gate, skirting round the house and tunnelling under a clematis arch.

above
Hornby clockwork
key that doubles-
up as a gauge for
ensuring rails are the
correct distance apart.
Unforgiveably I have
used Peco track below

below
Fyffes Banana Wagon,
Guard's Van, O Gauge
Tin Sign

One winding of the key would be enough for a loco and two trucks to travel the distance one way. So I was dispatched far out of sight to the front of the house to await the train. My excitement knew no bounds as I heard its approach, the train finally clattering slowly into view so that I could wind it up and send it back. The next time it appeared there was an apple for me sitting in the leading truck. On a fourth rewind I sent the core back, probably with a snail or two.

When we went on holiday by train to the Lincolnshire coast a short form version was parcelled up by my mother with that expert thing of making a string handle for ease of carrying. On rainy afternoons we set it up in the attic of the bungalow that sat precariously on a sand dune looking out to sea. Back home we never graduated to a Hornby Dublo electric train, and we wouldn't have swapped our clockwork dreams for one either.

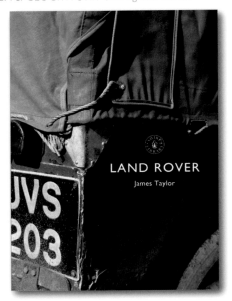

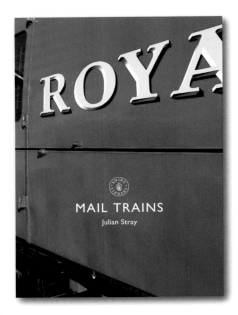

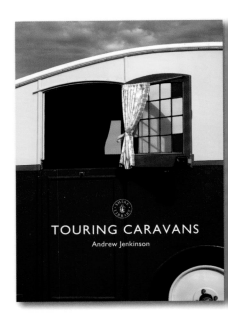

SHIRE BOOKS

above
A Shire classic
from 1986, first
published 1978

top
New covers
designed and
photographed
by the author

In Unmitigated England there are certain essential books that must appear on bookshelves. An assortment of Everyman Classics, a row of dog-eared Penguins, everything by Jonathan Meades and a set of Shell Guides. And there will always be at least a handful of Shire books. What an institution they have become: '…such gems' purred Joanna Lumley, '…in every way delightful' gushed Lucinda Lambton. And they're right. Perhaps we remember them as quirkily typographic booklets with monotone text and illustrations, telling us about hundreds of things from Whitby Jet to Roman Coins, but in 2007 they came under the brilliant direction of Nick Wright and the Shire brand was extended, pummelled into shape and made to stand upright in a smart new livery on its bookshop spinners.

Now I can no longer hide from telling you of my personal involvement. Six years on, Mr Wright and I met in a pub in Unmitigated England, and after surveying the landscape he said 'I might have a job for you'. What you see above, self indulgently, is the result of our making the subject of the books the hero (or heroine, depending). The new covers worked, they were liked, they moved things on. The trouble is that Shire's owners, it seems, had begun to lose interest, taking for granted the unique publishing icon in their care. You see they get excited over military books on guns 'n' stuff, which goes down really well in the USA, *naturellement*. But sadly I shouldn't think many members of the National Rifle Association get one on over Clarice Cliff.

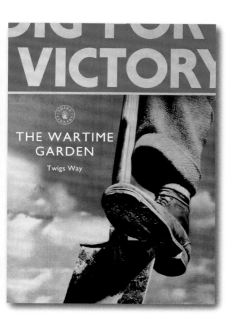

THE WARTIME
GARDEN

Twigs Way

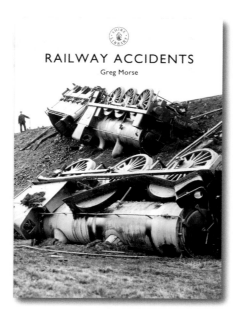

RAILWAY ACCIDENTS
Greg Morse

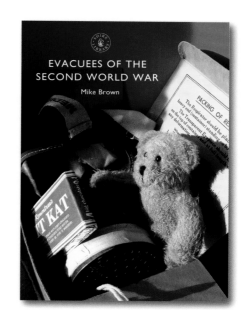

EVACUEES OF THE
SECOND WORLD WAR

Mike Brown

MECCANO
Roger Marriott

SHIRE LIBRARY

above
The new look
introduced in
2007

right
Items from *The
British Motor Industry
& Matchbox Toys*

Then an even bigger book maker came along and bought the tanks 'n' guns people. Poor old Shire didn't stand a chance and just about every single person who loved these books, and made them work very successfully, was told to pack up and go home. So now these brilliant books languish, like Sleeping Beauty, waiting for someone to give a well-deserved kiss of life to a very British institution. There is certainly no more eclectic and enjoyable a series of books than the Shire Library, and as such they should be valued by those responsible for them rather than carelessly pushed to one side. Where else will you find sheep with dentists, Victorian gardening next to touring caravans, smugglers with witches, medieval wall paintings next to Austin Sevens?

CAKES & ALE

COUNTRY MARKET TOWNS

Market towns came into existence in the Middle Ages, usually by consent of the ruling monarch and with the provision that they were a day's travel from each other. To begin with local produce would be sold in the churchyard after morning services, but in an essentially rural economy this grew into a fully-fledged market at the centre of what was now a town as opposed to a city or a village. Many took their name from this marketing privilege: Market Harborough, Market Drayton, Market Deeping, Market Weighton. And from the old Saxon word 'chipping' meaning 'to buy' we have Chipping Sodbury, Chipping Norton, Chipping Campden.

The location of markets was of course critical. They had to be convenient for both buyers and sellers. Where groups of people congregated was important, so they might easily get established at the junction of major roads or at river crossings. A market town would develop around a square or a wide street where stalls could easily be erected and dismantled, often grouped around a market cross. Flights of fancy in the extreme like Malmesbury, Winchester and Chichester, humbler canopies as in Dunster or Oakham. Many towns built market halls as a permanent building, although the wind could still blow through the open sides of those like Abingdon and Faversham. Later on other towns built more weatherproofed accommodation as can be seen in Devizes, Barnstaple and Newton Abbot.

Amazingly markets still survive in country towns. Whilst there is no longer a great demand for the offal and turnips of the medieval, your local market will nevertheless provide staples such as fresh vegetables, bread, fish and cheese. Equally my local one on a Friday helps me out with my bulk buys of batteries, dishcloths, shoe polish and clothes pegs. But my net is cast wider here with my selection of market towns, featuring more of the places themselves, where the character of the past still haunts the side streets as well as the market squares.

LARGE SIZE

Fresh picked peas

"A SANDRING
QUALITY
PRODUCT"

GARDEN PEAS

COUNTRY MARKET

These Choice English
Peas are canned within
a few hours of being
picked, and will be
found superior in
flavour to Fresh Peas
bought during the
Summer Season.

Open tin and empty
contents into a sauce-
pan and warm gently
for a few minutes when
they are ready to serve.

LARGE SIZE

Fresh picked peas

"A SANDRING
QUALITY
PRODUCT"

GARDEN PEAS

COUNTRY MARKET

These Choice English
Peas are canned within
a few hours of being
picked, and will be
found superior in
flavour to Fresh Peas
bought during the
Summer Season.

Open tin and empty

above
The Town Hall, 1678-82

above centre
Morlands Brewery plaque on The Old Anchor pub, St Helen's Wharf

above right
Sham ruins made from Abbey bits and pieces

right
Abbey Gateway detail

opposite
Streetscape showing the back of the Town Hall with the staircase tower

ABINGDON

Abingdon, despite the fact that the huge industrial city of Oxford is only six miles away, remains resolutely Berkshire. Not even the presence of the MG motor works…kills the essentially market and country quality of this meadow-set, river bordered, old brick town.

So wrote John Betjeman and John Piper, the editors of *Murray's Berkshire Architectural Guide* in 1949. How much has changed I wondered, having only been here once very early in the morning to snap the famous Town Hall. Now it's in Oxfordshire for some greyly bureaucratic reason, the MG works have disappeared entirely and Morlands brewery has been converted into flats. The A34 thunders monotonously by on the western borders, but the further you go eastwards towards the River Thames the better it becomes. In fact there is great pleasure to be had from wandering the streets, a jumble of architectural styles mostly not in competition but happily jostling along under a variety of pitched roofs.

The Abbey in Abingdon sat on the banks of the Thames, dissolved in 1538 and of which there is virtually no sign, like the car factory. Its outline is marked out like a grubby tennis court in a very municipal park, and various unrelated bits of it were put together as a sham set of arches and tucked away in a corner. But there is the fifteenth century gateway still extant, facing the late seventeenth century Town Hall that is a real showstopper. Built by Christopher Kempster, one of Wren's masons, it is typical of superb public architecture in the reign of Charles II. The Customs House in Kings Lynn comes immediately to mind. In 2007 I wrote that they were going to spend £5 million on a glass turret to house a lift up from the open market place underneath to the floor above. Thankfully sanity prevailed, and the space upstairs is now the Abingdon County Museum, still reached by stairs.

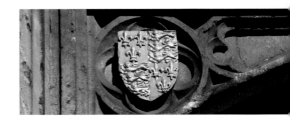

above
Incised and infilled with
black paint, the signage
for The Old Anchor

right
Brick Alley Almshouses,
1718

far right
Texture and colour,
a back yard off East
St Helen Street

below
Wood for the stove.
A narrow boat on
the Thames

below right
Pump clip from the
Loose Cannon Brewery

above
The Long Alley
Almshouses c1668

ABINGDON *(continued)*

All has not been as happily resolved with Abingdon's still standing medieval church of St Helen's. After seeing its noble spire soaring up over the river, and flying buttresses containing a five aisled interior that is broader than it is long, I went inside expecting to gasp with astonishment. And I did. Because the sun lit up very successfully rows and rows of hideous folding chairs and a scantily clothed altar that looked like it had come in a flatpack from Ikea. All on a tiled floor comprised of overs from a swimming pool job. Thankfully the church still sits in an environment little changed from early 20th century watercolours. South of the church there are more almshouses than old folk can shake their sticks at: The wonderfully named Twitty's (1707), the Long Alley where Pepys put 2/6 in the box in 1668 and the Brick Alley Almshouses of 1718 with arched balconies fenced in by white painted balustrades, the backs facing the river that is the one constant in Abingdon.

FAVERSHAM

Trace the north coastline of Kent eastwards from the Medway towns and you will arrive at the Isle of Sheppey, divided from the mainland by The Swale. Into this dividing water runs Faversham Creek, through which trade entered in and out of the town across Nagden Marshes. Trade which has left the memories of oysters, gunpowder, bricks, grain and flour still clinging on amongst black weatherboarded sheds and warehouses. And the ghost of Richard Arden who bought the dissolved Benedictine Abbey and was murdered by his wife and her lover in 1551. Authorship of the 1592 play *Arden of Faversham* has variously been accredited to amongst others Shakespeare and Marlowe, but is perhaps one of those truly anonymous dramas.

I always think Faversham divides into three very distinct parts. The East Kent Railway arrived to the south of the town in 1858, and after turning off either the M2 or the A2 you dog-leg through the result, a maze of Victorian terraces that form the first part and eventually bring you to the leafy outskirts of the second, the town centre with its very jolly 1574 Guildhall looking out over the market place. As with many traditional market halls of this kind the ground floor is open, showing to great effect the big timber arches. The surrounding streets still have many traditional shops, interspersed with antique and collectable emporiums that I always think manage to have artefacts I've never seen before, like odd shopfittings and sinister top-hatted mannequins.

FAVERSHAM *(continued)*

above
Standard Quay

above right
Boatyard crane

below
Recycled railway wagon

And so northwards into Abbey Street, a remarkable succession of pre-19th century houses and cottages, brilliantly and sensitively restored in 1961 by D.E. Nye & Partners with Anthony Swaine. Richard Arden lived at No. 80. The street leads up to The Anchor pub, where another quick dog-leg brings us to the third part and onto Standard Quay. Hopefully here will be a russet-sailed Thames barge held fast by thick ropes and probably leaning on the tidal mud. The exclamation marks here are the tall warehouse known as the 'Big Building' (1843-5), which hopefully still shows the ghost writing of 'United Fertilisers' and 'Oyster Bay House', and the imposing white rendered boarded-up house, the home of John Goldfinch, a foremost builder of sailing barges who had his yard next door. His most famous barge was the eponymous *Goldfinch*, launched c1894.

Further down the creek is home to a wonderful ramshackle world of make-do and mend. Almost a fourth part you may say. Boats on stilts waiting for maintenance, boats sinking into mud. Primary coloured cranes for hauling-up boats, disused rusty corrugated railway trucks for housing boat spares. Unmitigated pleasure. And the best of it all? Depending on the wind direction you will occasionally catch the very enticing evidence of good ales emanating from Shepherd Neame, Britain's oldest brewer (1698) at the heart of the town. Still fiercely independent, this is one of the best. I know, I've tested it many times.

above & centre
Shepherd Neame design

top
Faversham streetscape

right
Standard Quay with
John Goldfinch's house

FAKENHAM

above
Cyclists' Touring Club
plaque, Bridge Street

above centre
St Peter & St Paul
overlooking
the market

above right
Side street with
painted flint

below
Crowning glory
in the church

opposite
Goose eggs
from Smith's
of Gressenhall

Fakenham's a funny place. I don't mean that there's a clown on every street corner, but that it's one of those country market towns that has suffered in modern times and because of them. This would once of been a thriving centre at the heart of a very rural Norfolk community, the Thursday market day for outlying villages where Kettlestone would come for teapots, Little Snoring for bed linen and South Creake for hinge oil. Now the centre appears be receding against the usual tide of Tesco and Morrisons, and a big fire in 2014 didn't help when the wholesale destruction of the Aldiss store made an irreplaceable hole in the town centre. Aldiss as a furniture shop had in fact moved out of town to a 'superstore' leaving the building in the care of The Original Factory Shop. But the church of St Peter and St Paul still towers over the Market Place. I went in there and found the south aisle stuffed with books. I bought one on broadleaf trees with a cover illustrated by Charles Tunnicliffe for 50p and the lady who took my coin put it into a Next carrier bag and told me, 'There, you'll be really posh now'.

FAKENHAM *(continued)*

Just outside the church is a big red brick building that still speaks of leather-gaitered farmers coming in from wide Norfolk acres to do business. This is the Corn Hall of 1854-5 that became a bingo hall and is now the Central Cinema. From seed corn to pop corn. The great thing is, it still looks like a Corn Hall, and at least they were showing the latest *Far From the Madding Crowd*. The market itself has spread out into the fringes of the town centre, but I particularly liked the stalls gathered into the tight corners of the Market Place. The classic ingredients of town markets today: stacks of cauliflowers, boxes of tomatoes, coloured leads for dogs on one stall, hairy pigs' ears for them on another, bulk buys of firelighters and Colgate toothpaste. Eclectic and chaotic in equal measure, the only jarring note a hamburger van with its legend 'Get Stuffed' parked next to the war memorial.

above
Tooled-up in
Fakenham

above right
More eggs from
Gressenhall

right
Roses round
the door,
Hayes Lane

I got carried away with an orange trailer with let down sides that had brought eggs in from down the road in Gressenhall. I bought quails' eggs and an eye-wateringly big goose egg, and can vouch for the delights of the former if hard-boiled and washed-down with a decent champagne on a salt marsh in north Norfolk. I do hope Fakenham can recover and get back some of the rich spirit of its past. Market day is so obviously a high point, and possibly Fakenham suffers from having the market town of Holt just up the road, that has kept its small shops and local businesses intact. Too many market town centres drift remorselessly into bleak streetscapes of charity shops and little else. Now for that goose egg.

MELTON MOWBRAY

above
There are reputedly no Melton Mowbray pork pies to speak of made in the town now

left
Belvoir Brewery's 'Melton Red' beer bottle, the label also showing the magnificent tower of St Mary's parish church

'Painting the town red' would seem an unlikely phrase to be associated with this unassuming Leicestershire market town. A few miles down the road southwards is Lowesby Hall, home in the 1830s to the Marquis of Waterford. Hunting in those days also meant getting astonishingly trolleyed after the chase (or 'corked' as they would have said in understatement), and apart from making horses jump over dining room tables Waterford and his cronies decided to go to Melton to daub red paint everywhere. You can't see any evidence of this today unless it's equally mindless graffiti, but the legend is commemorated in the Belvoir Brewery's 'Melton Red' bottled beer. A typical rude comment in *The Guardian* said it was all nonsense anyway.

above
Natural Levain
Loaves and Fruit
Scones from the
Broughton
Bakery

above right
Auction Lots at
the Livestock
Market

Is it a myth? Difficult to say, after all you'd expect Melton Mowbray pork pies to be made here, since the fuss that was made over getting a 'Protected Designation of Origin'. But no, my Pie Spy tells me that apart from a few token ones made at the back of a shop, most are made fifteen miles away on an industrial estate in Leicester. By Ginsters apparently, alongside their 'Cornish' Pasties. Anyway, it's academic, as the best pork pies are made by a very individual butcher in Uppingham, Rutland. My unhumble opinion of course, but I have engaged in Pie Wars over them with a gamine girl from Halifax who claims the crusty crown for her native pinko variety. Melton does still have a Stilton creamery, one of only six able to bear the name.

If you knock on a local farmhouse door on a Tuesday morning looking for the farmer you are likely to be greeted by his wife / mistress / girlfriend telling you 'Oh no, he's gone to Melton'. This is because there's a livestock market, still next to the town centre. But before you get in amongst lowing cattle and bleating sheep, take a stroll through the street market. There's the usual stacking-up of household items with brand names you've never heard of, but very encouragingly I also discovered the Broughton Bakery where Laura Medhurst bakes organic bread, cakes and pastries out on a farm in neighbouring Nether Broughton and sells them in local markets. I bought two fruit scones before wandering in amongst the beasts.

MELTON MOWBRAY *(continued)*

above
Tuesday cattle
and sheep

below right
An auction in
progress

opposite
Clothes, tools
and a cockerel

We get here early. Well, early for us. By the time we're parking they're already hosing out cattle trucks and trailers and the market is simply buzzing (or mooing and crowing) with frenetic activity. One shed will have items for auction, which could be anything from a rusty lawn scarifier to table football, all scanned by practiced if jaundiced eyes. A 'butcher' with a microphone sells packaged meat at knock-down prices ('c'mon, bacon makes you live longer. It's a known fact that') and you can eat a heart-stopping breakfast roll whilst listening to him. There is much to occupy the eye, but still the main business is going on in the cattle ring and a big shed for 'fur and feather' where an auctioneer moves a little desk around between the cages and stacks of eggs.

Seeing cattle auctioned in a ring is to see a glimpse of Old England, a slightly frightening piece of bucolic theatre. Just don't show your ignorance like I did, thinking the prices were on the low side until being told despairingly, 'That's per kilo, Peter'.

DAFFODILS & MONSTERS

A PERSONAL NATURAL HISTORY

My father was a secret botanist. I don't mean he locked himself away from my mother in the shed to examine pistils and stamens, or, indeed, roam the countryside disguised as a curate but with a magnifying glass hidden in a recessed Bible. No, it's just that I didn't really recognise it, and wished I'd talked to him about it when he was still here. The biggest clue was a small book that he produced, *A Concise Glossary of Botanical Terms.* Purely a one-off, he hand drew all the listings from *achene* to *zygospore*. Where all this came from I have no idea. But there was a very large botanical atlas in the newspaper rack, always fought over when we played pencil and paper games at Christmas and needed something rigid to write on. Unfortunately this was taken too literally by someone, who underlined all the headings in this Victorian tome with a red biro. Haunting me over the years I recently managed to buy one, with its companion volume I never knew existed. Most must now be bought by certain art galleries for slicing-up into individual botanic prints.

I still don't really know my sepals from my follicles, but like much in nature that I enjoy it's the look of things. A clump of primroses under a sunlit hedge in springtime, a sinister group of toadstools in a dark wood. And it tends to be the flora rather than the fauna. Animals worry me, perhaps even frighten me a little. Perhaps it was seeing next door's dog fly through the air in order to kill a rat that had just run up inside our neighbour's trousers, or the something nasty in the wash house, as you will see. Birds are different. I put out the bits of bread slices that don't fit in the toaster for the jackdaws resident in neighbouring chimney pots, and look out for the first swallows returning to perch on the phone wires outside my office window.

So these short essays are mostly about the inanimate, the things I don't have to feed, be wary of (unless it's Deadly Nightshade) or worry about if I want to go on holiday. The joy of church flowers, spooky fungi and the fallen trees that metamorphose into monsters. Oh, and some chickens.

CHERRIES

PANSY

GOOSEBERRIES

POPPY

APPLE

SWEET PEA

PEAR

DAFFODIL

BLACKBERRIES

ASTER

STRAWBERRIES

PINK

PLUMS

POLYANTHUS

PEACH

TULIP

GRAPES

ROSE

IRIS

CHRYSANTHEMUMS

GARDEN FLOWERS

Our backyard met the back lawn by steps that had on either side what we called 'the grotto'. Sitting on the grass I was within earshot but out of sight of my mother who stood looking out from the open kitchen window. 'What's this plant called?' I shouted, fingering the leaves of a plant that grew with profusion over the stones. 'Mind your own business' came the reply, much to my confusion. It was some time before I understood the subtlety of common names for plants, but it's still a more thought-provoking name, or insult, than *Soleirolia soleirolii*.

Further adventures in this, to me, large garden came when I crawled down the path towards the oddball range of hen houses. Lupins towered above me like a guard of honour to my progress. As a result I still love them dearly, and was thrilled to find in recent years an old 35mm Kodak transparency of them in the rain, taken by my Aunty Rosalie. It made a change from her usual 'slides' which were pretty much exclusively of mud huts and banana trees in Nigeria where she was a missionary.

I was privileged to be surrounded by flowers then, as I am now. Although I must confess that it's my neighbours' efforts rather than my own (lawn, seat) that give me so much pleasure. Spring crocuses, summer hollyhocks and those strays from the surrounding countryside, magical foxgloves. The thundering blaze of the poppy, and still those lupins, still standing sentinel, so evocative and beautiful in evening sunlight.

79

Home. Back in England again.
A strange, still life. Everything misty. The low
green English countryside
unchanged. In the village church
always fresh flowers
on the altar…

Rebecca Foley in *Pravda* by
Howard Brenton and
David Hare

CHURCH FLOWERS

The heady scent greeting you at a church door can be intoxicating. Particularly if you arrive just before or after a wedding. So many times I have entered a cool dark interior on a summer's day to find ladies snipping at flower stems, offcuts strewn in the aisles and much puncturing of Oasis Floral Foam. Village chatter is kept *sotto voce* as one notices the plastic watering can perched on the tomb chest and green twine on the lectern.

Spring narcissi will trumpet against stained glass, a wonderfully abundant bouquet of exotic lillies will balance on a wrought iron stand next to the pulpit and window sills will disappear under variegated shades of greenery; hops are a favourite. Harvest Festivals see it all coming together, stalks of wheat made to look like they've just been taken from an old-fashioned stook, marrows and pumpkins jostling for position on the chancel steps.

I was very taken with the seemingly casual (in fact a great art) displays on the ledges of St John's church in Oxborough, Norfolk. Wild apples peeping out from behind blood red hips and papery seed cases. I then slowly became aware of a loud and very sinister humming noise and realised I was not alone. A congregation of wasps were reaching an orchestral crescendo as I fled into the churchyard.

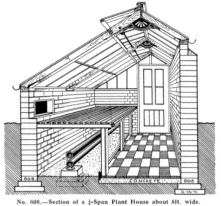

No. 608.—Section of a ½-Span Plant House about 8ft. wide.
used as an Intermediate Plant House or Stove House, Iron Stages as shown
page 112 are recommended, and more heating pipes are necessary.

above
Greenhouse,
Audley End, Essex

above centre
Watering cans,
Clumber Park,
Nottinghamshire

above right
Plant House diagram
from Messenger's
Catalogue c1920s

GREENHOUSES

Next door to my childhood home was a large Victorian house. It was odd in that the back door was on the same side of the front door, but at a suitable distance. This was reached by a driveway that separated the gardens of the two houses, and as soon as I could escape my own environment I imposed myself next door. This entailed pedalling my orange tricycle down the drive to where a greenhouse stood. The door was invariably open, and a voice from within would say 'Hello, Peter, what are you up to?' This was our neighbour, a kindly man in a green apron that had a cavernous pocket containing things like secateurs, twine and his Player's cigarettes. One of which always hung from his bottom lip. This was a completely alien world of heat, glass and the smell of damp soil and I loved it. My friend always explained what he was doing, intermittently coughing on the cigarette as his deft fingers prodded about in terracotta flower pots of varying sizes.

And once, as a treat, he showed me into a little adjoining brick shed where shelf upon shelf of wrapped apples waited in the dark.

So now I'll always try and get into a greenhouse, just to stand there and remember. The classic is of course a sloping roofed glass structure, possibly with an additional clerestory at the apex, the whole sitting on a brick-built base. Wooden stalls range down each side, hot pipes tucked underneath or cast iron gratings in the tiled or brick floor from which hot air rises into the steamy atmosphere. If I go to a typical country house for a day out I will irrevocably be drawn away from sun-shaded tapestries and roccoco furniture to the delights of a greenhouse. Or it could be an orangery, a peach house, a vinery for hot house grapes. For me cucumber frames, marrow forcing houses and melon pits have equal appeal. And then there's all the hardware.

above
Hothouse grapes,
Audley End, Essex

above centre
Window opening
mechanism, Clumber
Park, Nottinghamshire

above right
Peach catcher,
Audley End, Essex

below right
Clumber Park
Walled Garden and
Greenhouse

Winding gear for opening windows, cast iron sectional boilers. To say nothing of all those watering cans and trowels, and tucked out of sight a cut-grass scented Atco lawnmower sharing a gloomy shed with assorted wheelbarrows.

Glasshouses could easily be much bigger. Firms like Messenger & Co in Loughborough offered porches, conservatories, glazed verandahs and seaside winter gardens. Peach houses and forcing houses could be freestanding or utilise the wall of a kitchen garden, glass copings were made for protecting fruit trees against the same walls from frost. A letter from the Head Gardener at Hever Castle wrote to Messenger's in 1921: 'I have much pleasure in bearing testimony to the excellence of all the buildings which your firm carried out in these gardens'. I wonder if they were called in to look at the 1880

Camelia House at Nettlecombe in Somerset. Amidst an apocalyptic storm an eye witness recounted: 'It rose from the ground, filled with air like a crinoline, and fell, smashing into a thousand pieces'.

Such drama, one to stand alongside the storms of greenhouse conflicts in two films. First, and foremost, the greenhouse scene in Joseph Losey's *The Go-Between* (1971) where Leo Colston realises his nemesis has arrived in the form of the terrifying Mrs Maudsley, and the literally striking greenhouse scene in Norman Jewison's *In The Heat of The Night* (1967).

LANDMARK FIRS

above, left to right
East Norton,
Leicestershire

Meeting of the Gartree
Road and the River
Welland, near Ashley,
Northamptonshire

Goadby,
Leicestershire

Near Blyth,
Nottinghamshire

Wallend, Cumbria

opposite
Crossroads near
Cotterstock,
Northamptonshire

I was born in a house called 'The Firs'. It was late Victorian at the front, Georgian at the back, and this part would once have stood alone. In the front garden were two tall Scotch firs, and early on glorious summer mornings I would creep into my parents' bed and look out at the orange bark of one of them catching the first of the sun. Little did I know that decades later these trees would become something of another obsession.

It all started with Alfred Watkins' book *The Old Straight Track*. Written in 1925, it recounts Watkins' vision of straight lines connecting important topographic features in the landscape, and by the time of the 1970 reprint we were out there in the countryside with our maps, impossibly flared trousers and profoundly earnest looks on our faces. One chapter opened with this:

There is every reason to surmise that trees were planted in prehistoric times as sighting marks, although it is obvious that none so planted can now exist.

Indeed not, but their self-seeded progeny does. None more so perhaps than the Scotch fir, not a native species of the English landscape but used extensively as a marker because its tall evergreen silhouette remains constant throughout the year. But it was only ten years or so ago that I started to notice them in particular locations: crossroads, junctions, sometimes lonely inns. I obsessively ran about Leicestershire and beyond photographing them; they were, after all, easy to spot.

I've mentioned my 'discovery' to various compatriots whilst leaning on various pub bars, but so far my ramblings have been met with blank stares and remarks like 'Your round, Pete'. Drinking and Scotch firs. I now firmly believe, until scornfully told otherwise, that the bedroom in which I entered the world was upstairs in a drovers' inn, the trees marking its lonely presence from a distance.

POULTRY

Apart from the close proximity of my family, my early life appeared to have been shared with poultry. At the bottom of the garden was a set of higgledy-piggledy hen houses and wire netting, home to a range of hens scratching about around galvanised water troughs and grit dispensers. This demesne was my brother's, although my father insisted on dispatching them for the pot by beheading them with the firewood chopper round in the wash house. He once asked me if I'd like to see the execution. I agreed, but didn't expect the headless fowl to run off across the lawn back towards its erstwhile home. I can still see Dad now, removing the Player's from his lips to say, 'Well blow me'.

The huts were in constant need of maintenance, or so it appeared. One dull Saturday afternoon my chicken-owning brother decided to curry favour with my father by giving them yet another coat of preservative. The job had to done before my parents' return from Leicester and all was well until my brother ran across my father's precious putting green lawn with a bucket of creosote and tripped up. My other brother and I were up at my bedroom window with an air rifle and I learnt from him just one very useful but very prohibited expletive. It wouldn't have been so bad if the lawnmower hadn't been got out to try to remove the large brown stain from the grass. So on his return my father was greeted by the sight of a huge creosote star decorating his lawn and we had to endure an eerie silence for about a week.

Some years ago I came back to the remote gamekeeper's lodge we lived in to find one of the old Victorian dog kennels occupied by an unkempt brood of bantams. I had little to with them until one of the beasts decided to take against me. Very early on summer mornings it was my habit to wander aimlessly about bare-footed across the dew-soaked lawns. Until one day a fowl ran round the house and attacked me for no apparent reason. It then happened every time I dared to exit from the back door. Whatever the thing was doing it would stop and run at me, and as I write this my youngest son reminds me that he was up a tree in the orchard when

above
Welsummers, painted
by H. Hoyle for a
supplement to
The Feathered World
(1931)

right
Thorley Guide front
& back covers

bottom
Britains Hen & Chicks,
1970

one of these unprovoked attacks took place, and he, like me, learnt some inappropriate exclamations. I was just secretly glad when a fox got it.

The property bordered a large wood, and half-a-dozen guinea fowl were put into the depths by the gamekeepers as an alarm system to warn pheasants and partridges of impending danger. Well, that was the idea. They of course much preferred to nod about in the relative comforts of our garden, until Reynard had them too. I did miss Charlie though, an iridescently-feathered bantam cock who became a prop in my photographs of autumnal scenes, dutifully following carefully laid trails of corn.

FUNGI

above
The King Penguin
editions of *Edible Fungi*
& *Poisonous Fungi*.
The open page shows
Fly Agaric

below right
Sandringham Woods,
Norfolk

below
Field Mushrooms,
Hartley Wood, Kent

My first encounter with a proper toadstool was in Hyde Heath, up in the Chilterns above Great Missenden in Buckinghamshire. I was in trouble for hammering my uncle's bicycle pump connector to the model aeroplane I was making, and I wandered sullenly off across the road into the hinterland of a large beech wood. It was early morning, and the pale dewy grass seemed to tower over me until I was stopped in my tracks by a wondrous sight. All it needed was Big Ears to appear, for here was the storybook toadstool I now know to be a Fly Agaric. The classic red-top with white bits on it like flakes of cake icing, the books call it *Amanita Muscaria*, and it's poisonous, causing 'gastro-intestinal symptoms'. Ever since then I've been fascinated by all fungi, alongside a very healthy respect for them after a girlfriend and I ate some mushrooms I'd gathered from around the Lord Wantage monument near the Ridgeway, and we were, let's say, detained for some time.

More recently I have started photographing them, mostly not having a clue as to what they are. I just love the primeval sense they give off, the fruits of vast networks of mycelium suddenly appearing, literally overnight. It means being knee-deep in damp grass and dead leaves, and lying down waiting for the sun to highlight my subject. Which is why I caused great concern to a lady walking her dog in woods at Sandringham. 'Are you alright, dear?'

Probably my biggest surprise came in early autumn at Clipsham in Rutland whilst photographing a topiary avenue you'd expect to find in Alice's Wonderland. I was stepping backwards into the wood at the side and lost my balance. Tipping over into a shallow ditch I rolled over and saw a row of infant mushrooms on a bed of moss just catching the late afternoon sun that filtered through the branches overhead. I was reminded of that spooky Ray Bradbury story 'Boys! Raise Giant Mushrooms in Your Cellar!' and Derek Mahon's poem 'A Disused Shed in Co. Wexford'.

They always say you have to get up early to gather mushrooms, and you do around here because it's my neighbour you've got to be well ahead of. We both scan the fields for that fabulous delicacy the Giant Puffball (*Calvatia gigantea*). Cutting it open should reveal thick, hard, white flesh. Don't eat anything that isn't, and if it's the real thing just lightly fry both sides of a thinnish slice. As soon as you can.

MONSTER FIELDS

above
'Please don't eat me!'
Obeisance is
made near
Hartley Wood,
Kent

top
Knole Park, Kent

above right
Anguished Ash,
next to the Eye Brook
on the Leicestershire-
Rutland border

One snowy morning I was driving across to Uppingham in Rutland. As I crossed the county boundary with Leicestershire on a bridge over the Eye Brook, I noticed that a majestic ash tree by a field gate had been felled. The 'tree surgeons', or whoever, were obviously in the process of cutting it up for the local woodburners, but resting from their labours for the weekend had left this monster rearing up on his (one assumes) front legs. A few days later he had gone, leaving just a snow-covered stump by the hedge. As I pondered the photograph I'd taken, a distant bell rang concerning the artist Paul Nash.

In 1931 Margaret Nash bought her husband a Kodak pocket camera. As the asthma he suffered from took hold he increasingly relied on it as, he said, 'another eye'. In 1939 he wrote an essay on felled trees looking like monsters, and photographed a sample in 1940 which he entitled *Monster Field*. This turned into a booklet limited to 1,000 copies, with the text a facsimile of his handwriting, a watercolour on the cover and more monochrome photographs. Nash died in the year of its publication, 1946.

above
Crawling back to his lair, Hartley Wood, Kent

above top
One in the bush worth two in the hand. East Carlton Park, Northamptonshire

above right & below
Two ancient specimens in Knole Park near Sevenoaks in Kent

The Anguished Ash started my quest to find my own specimen creatures. Looking like gargantuan mutating stick insects, they are rarely seen in dense woodland, being so well camouflaged. No, they like to take up their gaunt poses in open fields, often parkland where hopefully they are allowed to graze unmolested without fear of imminent chainsaw massacres. Knole, just outside Sevenoaks in Kent, provided a happy hunting ground to discover woodfaces staring out from amongst the vegetation.

LANDSCAPE FLOWERS

'A patchwork quilt' is in some parts still a useful metaphor for the variety of colour in English fields and roadsides. Post harvest pale yellow stubble, the earthy brown of recently ploughed fields, acres of fresh green vegetables, buttercup-starred meadows. But every now and then our senses are assaulted by a palette that sends artists reaching for under-used tubes of paint and photographers screeching to a halt to poke their cameras over a hedge or field gate.

The unmissable colour is of course when almost overnight the countryside is splashed with the acid yellow of rape flowers, contrasting so much with dark hedges and skies. I used to think they were mustard fields, and thought that Colmans in Norfolk must produce far more than is mythically left on the side of plates. But no, round here they're the flowering heads of oil seed rape,

tiny black ball-bearing like seeds variously giving us posh cooking oils, fine lubricants and fodder for livestock. Apiarists sometimes grind their mandibles because bees just love it, the trouble being that it gives a taste of honey not always appreciated. As it increases in our fields, so does this member of the cabbage family escape from the fields to casually colonise headlands and roadsides.

Fields of red poppies are of course very emotive. Has any other flower such immediate and almost visceral power? Although seeds have been found in archaelogical digs dating far back in time, a symbol of disturbed earth and agricultural regeneration, it is as a symbol of the loss in the First World War that is perhaps top-of-mind. Although even during the conflict soldiers were using them to make gardens in the trenches.

above left
Fields of rape between Hallaton and Horninghold in Leicestershire

above right
Rape flower near Bringhurst, Northamptonshire

opposite
Poppies near Bringhurst

LANDSCAPE FLOWERS (continued)

Poppies are amongst the most difficult wild flowers to photograph, immediately wilting on being picked. Photographer Tony Evans was asked by Penguin books for an image to go on the covers of *First World War Poetry*, and memorably went out early one morning, dug a patch up and drove back to his studio whilst his assistant kept the clump watered in the back of the van, until they could be shot against a black background.

The moment that cow parsley billows out on the roads and lanes around here a yellow contracting tractor with a big arrow on the back revs-up and starts to cut it all down. The council will repeat a mantra about road safety and visibility, but surely if you can't see round the corner on a country lane you should slow down anyway. Cow Parsley, Queen Anne's Lace, Badman's Oatmeal, Grandpa's Pepper. Different names in different countrysides, (I remember my father pointing to it with a driving-gloved finger and just saying 'keck'), this flower is so ebullient in May, obscuring field gateways and signpost names alike. Or very simply just looking good stuffed in a convenient receptacle on a kitchen table.

above left
Photography of poppies for a Penguin book by Tony Evans

above right
Signpost in Weston-by-Welland, Northamptonshire

The place-names all hazed over...

MCMXIV
Philip Larkin

For a long time I puzzled over a roadside plant that proliferates in Norfolk. Or, more particularly, as I got nearer to the coast. They are I discovered *Smyrnium olustratum*, or Alexanders. The Romans used every bit of the plant for everything, and probably introduced it here. One can imagine an amphora of seeds being cracked open at their fort on the North Norfolk coast at Brancaster. Richard Mabey tells us it's worth trying the thicker stems to eat, cooking it like celery, the plant that succeeded it in eighteenth century cottage gardens.

BLACK & WHITE

ENGLAND IN MONOCHROME

above

Ilford HP3
photographic film.
Develop before
1958

opposite

How it used to
be for our black
and white
snapshots.
An exposed film
handed in at a
chemist or
photographic
shop, a couple
of days wait
followed by a
nervous flick
through the
results outside
on the pavement

I joined a photographic club at school, and spent many happy hours locked in a big store cupboard that doubled-up as a darkroom. Developing, enlarging, printing, I emerged smiling if reeking of chemicals. That was until the rubber hose that was connected to a tap so that constant running water could flow through a big Belfast sink decided on a whim to make a bid for freedom in order to start flooding the floor instead. In my absence it continued to do so until water ran down the walls of the chemistry storeroom underneath, to startling effect.

These were black and white days indeed. I only really saw colour in print when I looked at a Spangles ad in *Picture Post* magazine, and cinema films dazzled me if they were in Technicolor. To a post-war boy the war had been in monochrome, and it's still disconcerting to see colour footage of dark green Lancasters and Adolf Hitler in boy scout biscuit-coloured khaki. It's as if someone's made it up, and sometimes they have. Slowly colour wound in and out of our Kodak Brownies, and that became the norm. But some of the great photographers stuck with black and white, perhaps because in monochrome a subject is more easily assimilated, there's less to distract. A picture of a red brick cottage with pink roses round a green door becomes a cottage with roses round the door. If you see what I mean.

In the 1950s books on England were invariably full of monochrome pictures, with perhaps a token colour shot on the cover. I think this was because colour printing hadn't really caught up; what looked good on a Kodachrome transparency lost something if one of the four process colours used in printing was only fractionally out of register. Now of course we've achieved so much more, although printing still doesn't quite match what we see on our backlit digital screens. But the techno revolution does mean we can take pictures in monochrome again, or even drain our colour shots, without locking ourselves in the dark with bottles of evil smelling chemicals, unless we want to.

THE CORONATION OF JOHN RAVEN-HILL

above left
Marble Arch

above right
Westminster Abbey

below right
A Coronation biscuit
tin and Park Lane

opposite
Dean's Yard
Westminster

below
John Raven-Hill, c1953

In 1953 John Raven-Hill was living in Richmond in Surrey. I know this because his three gorgeous daughters are very well known to me. So when I saw these photographs of his visit to London sometime over the Coronation period they stopped me in my tracks. This is what can happen to photography sometimes, that the focus within a picture can change dramatically over time. Like seeing a picture of the Queen and years later noticing that one of your mates is grinning in the background. John thought he'd photographed buildings, I'm glad he photographed traffic.

John was positioning his viewfinder on The Sanctuary, Sir George Gilbert Scott's 1854 building in Dean's Yard to the west of Westminster Abbey, and whoosh! a Humber Pullman limousine speeds by to grab my attention sixty years later.

Marble Arch is transformed by a Bedford confectionery truck, a humpty-back Standard Vanguard, a Fordson van. And Kia-Ora. Pre- and post-war Vauxhalls pose in front of the west front of the Abbey, with an Albion lorry. The hotel below is the Dorchester on Park Lane, with an accidental two-tone Armstrong Siddeley Sapphire and RT bus. Maybe John meant to do all this; he certainly would say he did.

COUNTRY LIFE PICTURE BOOKS

above
Kersey, Suffolk

below
Country Life
Book Colophon

As one would expect of a high class country magazine, the quality of the Country Life Picture Books was excellent. Printed on art paper, they concentrated on carefully taken photography with the minimum of text, although taunting the potential customer with full colour photos stuck separately on the bright covers. They came with a map overwritten with the page numbers, and each volume had fifty eight photographs by well-known lensmen like A.F. Kersting.

G.F. Allen's photograph of Tideswell near Miller's Dale, entitled 'The Cathedral of The Peak' from the Peak District volume (1961) is typical, an anecdotal image that is more than just a pretty picture of a church tower. The season is announced with heavy blossom, and we are reminded of a forgotten age when at a certain time everyone would light their fires in readiness for tea at four o'clock. Or was that just in Tideswell?

From the East Anglia edition (1958) I like the photograph of Kersey in Suffolk with the bulbous Austin Somerset negotiating the watersplash, watched over by a spectator who is perhaps hoping for the photographer (J. Allen Cash) to get a good soaking. Number 50 in the same volume shows the Moot Hall captured by Donovan E.H. Box in Steeple Bumpstead, Essex. And in case you think I've made that up we once lived in a remote farmhouse near here and were given the telephone number for our new Trimphone as 'Steeple Bumpstead 369'. Nowadays it would be like living in Midsomer.

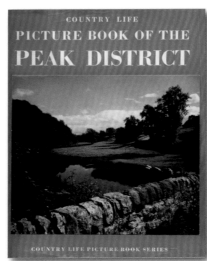

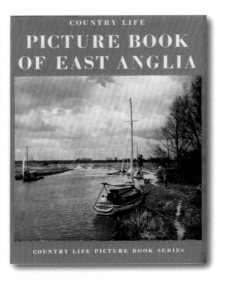

above
Tideswell,
Derbyshire

above right
The Moot Hall,
Steeple Bumpstead,
Essex

right
Two Country Life
Picture Books.
The colour pictures
were printed
separately and then
glued on

ERIC DE MARÉ

Eric De Maré was one our foremost architectural photographers. I first came across his work when I was putting together a little book on canals, and his 1950 *The Canals of England* opened-up a watery world of lock weirs, cast iron bollards and atmospheric canalside pubs. The first thing I noticed was that De Maré didn't just turn up and press the shutter. His pictures are obviously a record of buildings but many go beyond the archival. Here I can almost smell the aromas of Bullards in Coslany Street Norwich, and I'm thankful that their Anchor Brewery building has survived for new purposes, albeit without the landmark chimney. His photograph of Brighton isn't a straight-on view of a stuccoed streetscape, it's a narrative of how we come across these places, an exuberant corner statement with the crescent receding in the background. This 1888 tin tabernacle is still with us, re-erected at Blists Hill Victorian Town in 1977.

De Maré was born in 1910 in Enfield, and in the late 1940s undertook a series of commissions to document our industrial heritage. Anonymous warehouses around canal basins, vast Gloucestershire textile mills and the new power stations reconfiguring the landscape. A body of work that is a now a unique and invaluable insight into the vernacular and ordinary.

Spitalfields Market, London

Castle Acre, Norfolk

Slaughden, Suffolk

Battersea Power Station, London

Birling Gap, East Sussex

Highley, Shropshire

awston, Leicestershire

Porthleven, Cornwall

arkton, Northamptonshire

Beddingham, East Sussex

xborough, Norfolk

Church Langton, Leicestershire

ODHAMS PRESS

Picture books by Odhams were so ubiquitous in the 1950s and 60s that every secondhand bookshop will have at least a couple on their shelves. Now considered very old fashioned, particularly when placed against the seemingly faultless digital imagery of today, I nevertheless think that they have a valued place in the bibliography of English topographical books. Odhams were essentially magazine publishers who in 1937 moved into an Owen Williams designed print hall in Watford, that with its clock tower looks from some angles like a modernist Baptist church. The last title to come off the thundering presses was *Smash* magazine in the New Year of 1969.

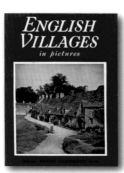

The books were cosily English. In *The New Forest and Hampshire*, in uncredited pictures photographers exposed their monochrome films on stands of trees, stacks of timber, rural crafts and rural pastimes. Occasionally a remembrance bell is struck, as in the photograph of The Royal Oak pub in the Forest at Fritham, although the book omits the inn's name. Strong of Romsey had a staggering 940 pubs when they were bought by Whitbread in 1969, but brewing ceased in 1981. So no longer can we enter 'Strong Country', but we can still think about this hot afternoon with the casually placed bicycles and Fritham dogs. You can almost hear the murmur of conversation inside.

English Villages remembers olde Englishe customs like hanging boys upside down over marker stones in Plymstock's 'Beating the Bounds' ceremony in western Devon, and Honiton in the same county's 'Hot Money' on Fair Day which appeared to mean you had to put your head down a drain. A less doubtful activity in Buckinghamshire was driving cattle over the village green in Chenies, past a London Country bus stop. I'd like that still to happen.

JAMES RAVILIOUS

above
Bill Hammond
thatching a rick,
Westacott,
Riddlecombe.
August 1986

opposite top
Felling a dangerous
elm at Down Farm,
Dolton. September
1975

opposite bottom
Dairy churns,
Hatherleigh.
February 1976

I sit absorbing James Ravilious's photographs more than anyone else's. This isn't *Countryfile*, telling us we can only really enjoy landscapes by abseiling down them, but the very real, sometimes harsh countryside of North Devon, inhabited by equally unpretentious people: farm labourers uprooting an elm with a Field Marshall tractor; a lone soul against the sky thatching a rick. Or sights we will probably never see again: as the sun struggles through the clouds, empty churns lie scattered around a roadside platform, their random angles telling of a recent drop-off. Like a superb film, I am always drawn into something beyond Ravilious's actual photography, into the atmosphere of the moment.

The surname will of course be familiar; James' father was the artist Eric Ravilious. With his wife Robin (the daughter of glass-engraver Laurence Whistler) he left London for a small cottage in Dolton, North Devon. He became an 'artist in residence' at the Beaford Art Centre, and embarked on recording the rural life in an area of around ten miles of the village. Initially part-time the project became all-consuming. With his 35mm Leica with pre-war uncoated lenses and customised lens shade he patiently exposed film to record countless rural scenes, simple cottage interiors and the lives of North Devon people. His work ranks amongst the very best, and deserves to be known much more widely.

LOBSTERS & LILOS

ENGLISH SEASIDES

above
Crabs, anchors and
parasols. Symbols
of an English
seaside

opposite
The deckchair,
municipal
essential

In the early 1950s special trains would leave for Skegness and the Lincolnshire coast from the now vanished Belgrave Road station in Leicester, and it was here, lit by an early morning sun, that we embarked eastwards. We finally decanted at Mumby Road and then filled a big black Austin taxi that took us over the green fields until we could see a row of bungalows perched against the sky at Anderby Creek, halfway between Chapel St Leonards and Sutton-on-Sea. This would be our home for the next few weeks, and running across a wooden verandah and jumping down into warm white sand is my earliest memory of a holiday.

At first it was always the east coast. After Lincolnshire it was Norfolk, either head to toe in a caravan or arriving by steam train at halts from where we walked through poppies and wheat to the sea and a cliff-top bungalow. The big breakthrough came in 1959 when we adventured across London to Charing Cross and into a green electric train that hummed down to Sandling in Kent, from where we went down a lane in a squeaky Bedford

coach to Hythe. A whole new world opened up. Seeing the first Mini in a Folkestone showroom, travelling by the Romney Hythe and Dymchurch Railway to Dungeness, canoeing down the Royal Military Canal with my father. And then the grumpy teenage years of glaring out from the back seat of my father's apple green Ford Popular as we took all day to go to the Yorkshire coast at Whitby, the only compensation my wearing black suede winklepickers and playing Beatles records on café jukeboxes.

Anderby Creek was never the same after the 1953 floods left our bungalow leaning like a nervous diver on the sandbank, so the pleasures of eastern England spread to the North Norfolk coast and down into Suffolk, and Whitby grew in my estimation. My mother doubtless gave my winklepickers to the dustmen, but thanks to parents that took the trouble to take a noisy toddler and a recalcitrant youth on holiday, I am now passionate about the English coast. Brash resorts, atmospheric beaches, fresh lobsters, I'm continually wandering towards the edge.

BRIGHTON

Somewhere in a family album is a photo of my Aunty Edie and Aunty Daisy sitting on a promenade seat eating ice creams. Both are wearing big cloche hats over their eyes and laughing their heads off. It's probably 1930, but it's definitely Brighton. How I wanted to go there instead of shivering on the Lincolnshire coast, but in our household the name of this Sussex seaside resort was said in the same way as they went on to say 'Christine Keeler'. All so unfair, but I suppose to a post-war generation it was still the Brighton of Graham Greene's 'entertainment' *Brighton Rock*. London's low life, down for racecourse muggings, Pinkie sharpening his razor under the pier, the smell of gas in peeling stuccoed apartments, Kolley Kibber leaving his prize winning cards under teashop table cloths. But has it really all disappeared? I don't think so, as Keith Waterhouse so aptly said: 'Brighton is a town that always looks as if it is helping police with their inquiries'.

As soon as the electric train emerges from under the South Downs at the Clayton Tunnel and runs over the Preston Park viaduct you are soon inside the magnificent Brighton trainshed and exiting from under the giant clock still initialled with 'London, Brighton & South Coast Railway'. Just as countless racegoers in trilbys have done, murderers with torsos in cabin trunks, Laurence Olivier and Dora Bryan glancing up at it as they alighted from the Brighton Belle luxury train. Always with the incessant scream of gulls over the ornate roof.

above
The Royal Pavilion,
1815-22

right
Southdown bus
shelter on the
Old Steine

far right
Seaside staple
diet, sponsored
by dentists

Brighton as a resort started with the Prince of Wales and his entourage finding a way through the Downs to the little fishing town of Brighthelmstone in the 1780s. Boats drawn up on the shingle, narrow doubtful alleys now called The Lanes. At first they didn't stroll along the seafront, but wandered about on the common land of The Steine, soon to be looked out over from Nash's fantastic remodelling of the Prince's guest house into the Royal Pavilion (1815-22). Onion domes, pagoda roofs, finials, friezes; it is impossibly exotic. 'Hindoo' they called it.

THE "VICTORY".

BRIGHTON *(continued)*

The seafront mansions, the crescents, squares and terraces soon followed, the town developing to the west (Hove, actually, as they say) and to the east with Kemp Town. The railway came, London came. Eugenious Birch's West Pier arrived in 1863-6, the Palace Pier thirty years later. The latter is still there with seafood and a helter skelter, the West Pier now just a devastated starling-haunted wreck out in the waves, a ghastly monument to red tape and utter neglect.

This iron ghost should be put to rest, but if you want to see just how good it was, look at Richard Attenborough's directorial debut *Oh! What a Lovely War* (1969). This Len Deighton scripted film used the pier as a surreal background to key events in the First World War. A Brighton refuse tip served as the trenches and cast-iron columned Madeira Drive as an unadulterated seaside promenade. The Downs were put to spectacular use in the unforgettable final scene.

Come on Algernon
That's not enough for me.
Give me some more
The same as before,
Because I can't count under three.
Give me a tip top stick of Brighton rock
And how I'll coo.
None but a whopping one
A topping one,
Algy there's simply no stopping one.
Give me just another one do.

From the Ealing Studios film *Champagne Charlie* (1944). Words by T.E.B. Clarke, music by Lord Berners

WESTON-SUPER-MARE

above
The terraces of
Knightstone Road
with St John's church
and Worlbury Hill

above right
Carter's Steam Fair's
Morris ice-cream van

below
Donkey work on
the beach

opposite
Austin J40 pedal car
adapted for a Carters
Steam Fair ride. They
were made by disabled
Welsh miners from
offcuts of the full size
Austin Devon & Dorset

'The insistent charm of Weston-super-Mare is in large measure due to the natural beauty of its setting, cradled in the arms of wooded Worlbury Hill and the grass-clad height of Brean Down…' So wrote Maxwell Fraser in her Somerset guidebook for the Great Western Railway in 1934. I didn't quite know what to expect on my visit, but I have to say it was a very pleasant surprise. And the decent weather helped. Weston is the first resort of any size, with perhaps the exception of Clevedon, that lies on the Somerset coast below Bristol. It's where the Severn becomes the Bristol Channel, so when the tide goes out you can encounter estuarine mud. You won't notice it at first because you'll be gazing out at the islands of Flat Holme and Steep Holme, seven or so miles out, and across to the coast of South Wales at Barry.

Weston was a collection of fishermen's huts in 1819 when Dr Johnson's friend Mrs Piozzi visited. She commented that 'the breezes here are most salubrious' and that is certainly still true. There are now the usual delights associated with the Day Out, but I loved the setting, and the fact that Carter's Steam Fair was here on the seafront with their classic rides and ice cream served from a converted Morris J2 van. It made the slog down the M5 even more worthwhile.

117

ALDEBURGH

Rarely does the imagined match up to the reality, but in this Suffolk seaside town it gets pretty near. If one is looking for 'The Borough' of Benjamin Britten's *Peter Grimes* one may be a little disappointed, but only because the butcher, baker and candlestick maker appear to have been replaced by Joules, Crew and Jack Wills, those identikit and ubiquitous comfort zones of Middle England. Aldeburgh does indeed move with the restlessness of the tides that sweep up and down the shingle, but much remains that keeps me coming back ever since I accidentally made Britten bang his head on the boot lid of his Alvis convertible in 1968.

E.M. Forster called it 'a bleak little place, not beautiful' and I suppose on a dull wintry afternoon with an easterly wind blowing onshore this could be true. But Forster still loved it as I do, and to walk along the beach early on a summer's morning from the White Lion Hotel to the Martello Tower at Slaughden is impossibly romantic. The neat terraces of ice-cream coloured houses looking out to sea from the Crag Path, counterpointed by the detritus of fishing: a couple of boats drawn up on the shingle, rusty hausers, stacks of fish boxes and neat lettering announcing the morning's catch.

The lifeboat painted by Eric Ravilious is now housed in a state-of-the-art structure, but the two look-out towers of the rival beach companies that once competed for salvage are still here just as we see them in Kathleen Hale's Orlando the Marmalade Cat's *A Seaside Holiday*. Hale called it Owlbarrow, and it's easy to see in her coloured lithographs that Aldeburgh makes a very satisfying subject for painters, and indeed has became an inspiration for many writers from the poet Crabbe to authors H.G. Wells, Thomas Hardy, M.R. James (who called it Seaburgh), and of course musicians, much evidenced by Benjamin Britten.

Aldeburgh is on the sea, but isn't a resort as such; there are no promenades, no amusement arcades, no laughing sailors in glass cases. The Moot Hall is the perfect exhibit to demonstrate how the town used to be. This 16th century timber framed, flint and herringbone brick building with its exterior staircase was once not only a market hall and courtroom but also in the middle of the town, the eastern half of which is now under the waves. Such is coastal erosion here in Suffolk, even more dramatically seen (or not seen) at Dunwich where I saw the last piece of the last of eight or nine parish churches disappear into the sea in 1969.

ALDEBURGH *(continued)*

above & above right
An Antony Gormley
sculpture, one of five
celebrating 50 years
of the Landmark Trust,
1965-2015, and the
Martello Tower on
which he stands

top & above centre
Aldeburgh Moot Hall
and detail

top right
King Street houses

They say that the spit of land to the south of
the town at Slaughden, between the River
Alde and the sea, may be allowed to be finally
breached by the waves. Leaving in isolation
the most northerly Martello Tower on the
English coast. On my latest visit the tower,
erected to defend the coast against possible
Napoleonic invasion, had a temporary
Antony Gormley figure standing on the
roof, surveying the landscape that may soon
irrrevocably change. It is from this viewpoint
that one can best see the vulnerability of this
fragile coastline, the sea to the left, the town
in front, marshes to the right.

The shrill calls of gulls over rooftops and
fishing boats, the cry of curlews over creeks
and marshes, all find their echo in the music
of Benjamin Britten. With Peter Pears he
founded the Aldeburgh Festival in 1948,
and although the old maltings at Snape are
its musical home now, it is still Aldeburgh
that resonates not only with refrains and
recitatives but all that goes with them, a
cultural atmosphere with a character unlike
any other. Ben and Peter with hesitant
pints of Adnams in their hands, John and
Myfanwy tucking into fish 'n' chips, Imogen
and Mstislav dipping their toes in the sea.

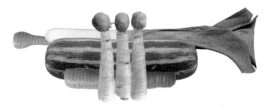

CORNWALL

The black and white Cornish flag is only a few steps away from being a Jolly Roger. Highly appropriate for a county that sets itself apart from the rest of England, regarded by many as a haunt of smugglers with lanterns on dark nights, wreckers with lanterns on even darker nights and Poldark scything his clifftop to a chorus of sighs. The Reverend Hawker praying for drowned sailors in Morwenstow, Daphne Du Maurier evoking the smell of tobacco still on the air after a piratical ship has left *Frenchman's Creek*. All helping to distil the essence of memory that separates the realities of failed tin mines and over-regulated fishing from what have become quintessentially romantic English holidays. There isn't the space here to do Cornwall the justice that it so richly deserves, so I'll just set a few pointers down that relate to places that have a particular plangency for me.

Although Cornwall has a hinterland of hidden farms, narrow lanes lined with stunted trees bent by westerly storms and a prehistoric landscape map-pinned by standing stones, menhirs and fougous, once again I always want to be looking out to sea. Along with everybody else. To the south of St Agnes is Chapel Porth, reached down a narrow lane that ends at a National Trust car park where you can buy hedgehog ice creams. Below the gaunt remains of Wheal Coates mine that opened in 1872, closing in 1914, is a beach edged with the dark openings of caves that reach into the unfathomable interiors of the cliff. (For extraordinary views from inside the caves looking out you could do no better than to take a look at the paintings of Sarah Adams.) The beach itself always invites the thought that after every high tide one can walk on sand unmarked by anyone else, ever.

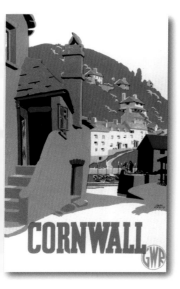

The same idea occurs to the north of
St Agnes at Trevaunance Cove, reached
down a lane descending through the trees
to the Driftwood Spars Hotel where doggies
are very welcome and surfers wetsuits dry
in the sun. Probably. Walk up to the clifftop
here and look out to sea where the two rocks
mysteriously called 'Man and His Man' sit
catching the waves.

Building a harbour here in 1793 to service
the tin mines was accomplished with a huge
amount of effort, but over the last eighty
years or so all trace of it has now vanished.
Remnants of the industry are still scattered
over the cliffs, with a sensitively restored
mine engine house presiding over all. Beware
of incoming tides down below, the beach
completely disappears.

CORNWALL *(continued)*

Further to the east Perranporth can get very busy, but on a bright October day it is a singular pleasure to walk out from the town on the beach northwards up to Penhale Sands. If you're lucky there will be nobody else near, and you can turn off the wide expanses of sand and rummage about as I did trying to find the shrine of St Piran's Oratory, the remains of which are buried in the dunes marked only by a nearly invisible marker stone. St Piran is the patron saint of tinners (there are lots of saints in Cornwall) and he floated across from Ireland on a millstone. Apparently. After founding his baptistery he dug his own grave, occupying it in AD 550.

above
Porthleven on
the south coast
of Cornwall

right
Porthleven from
above the eastern
side of the
harbour. Top left
by the jetty is the
very agreeable
Ship Inn

Porthleven was a fishing village where in the 1930s you could still watch ships being laden with granite and indeed ships being built. In 2014 the sea did what it always wants to do; see how much damage it can cause. On my visit to the town the year before this characterful south Cornish coast harbour was relatively tranquil, but still with big seas washing noisily around the walls and jetties. The next February the biggest storm for ten years crashed into the harbour, ripping out the lock gates and destroying six fishing boats. This is the Cornwall of legend, with a wildly unpredictable sea that painter Maggi Hambling says can be 'a roaring raging beast'.

left
A 1937 'Balloon'
Blackpool tram

above
From the top: Tower
World, Canopy lettering
at the Grand Theatre,
and Noah's Ark at the
Pleasure Beach

BLACKPOOL

What I found surprising about Blackpool is that there is so much more to it than the famous all-singing all-dancing seafront and the immediate hinterland of landladies and candlewick bedspreads. You could get to the end of the M55 and lose yourself in a tangle of back streets, find Blackpool Airport tucked in between the town and Lytham St Anne's and with a bit of luck discover the Premium Bond 'factory', as a Lancastrian pub landlord once described it to me. To the north is Fleetwood, and it's to here that the famous cream and green trams run. They are one of the best bits for me, not really being a slot machine candy floss sort of bloke. The railway arriving in the 1840s brought the holiday-makers surging in from northern mill towns, the Eiffel Tower lookalike was opened in 1894 and lit up like a Christmas tree

as part of the famous illuminations. Hiram Maxim's Captive Flying Machine arrived at the Pleasure Beach in 1904 (bits of it are still there), Ken Dodd got his tickling stick out and Alan Bradley got run over by a tram chasing Rita in *Coronation Street*. To get the full-on Blackpool flavour that's not just novelty rock, tattoos and 'avin a larf, watch the eponymous television series *Blackpool* (2004) and the extraordinary *Funland* (2005).

Both a long way from the fishing village on the Fylde coast looking out over the Irish Sea.

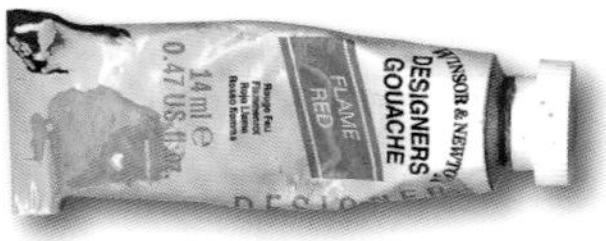

PIPES & PAINT

DESIGN WITHOUT A MAC ON

above
Designers Gouache. Add water, use brush

opposite
'Commerce & Prosperity' 1951 Festival of Britain stamps by Edmund Dulac (1882-1953)

In 1963 a little book caught my eye called *Graphic Design: Visual Comparisons.* It was written by the newly-formed London design group of Alan Fletcher, Colin Forbes and Bob Gill. Gill was from New York and Fletcher had just been there, back from the city that was transforming how we thought about advertising and design. This was the *Mad Men* era of witty ideas beautifully expressed, and the examples in the Fletcher Forbes Gill book set my head spinning. Because it so obviously wasn't just about being able to draw (although that undoubtedly helped), but about solving problems simply and creatively.

Oh how I fell to earth when I arrived at my first job in what was still called a commercial art studio. When I got out a Magic Marker I was told to put it away and start mixing paint. 'When I started the bloody pencil was still on the secret list' I was told. But I did learn, painting all my visuals before finally graduating to markers and Letraset. I learnt to hand-draw lettering, to mark up layouts for a typesetter, to make tea and empty dustbins. Learning to walk before I finally ran. I'm so glad it was this way. Just being able to draw lettering gave me a discipline that has, hopefully, stayed with me. As has the humour and the sense of the absurd that I witnessed from such a disparate set of characters in the studio. Mad men in the very best sense of the words.

So this chapter is about design before the computer. When everything was created with handmade visuals turned into print via sheets of artboard, pens and brushes. Here you will find my design heroes together with some things I've collected over the years. Every designer does that, drawers full of stuff that might be of use one day. I kept my FFG book and after listening to an interview session with them in the old Billingsgate Fish Market I vaulted over all the seats and got them to sign it. I proffered the book to Alan Fletcher first. 'Have you got a pen' he gruffly required. I patted my pockets to find I hadn't. 'Call yourself a designer' he said, getting out a Rotring pen and drawing, rather than writing, the word 'Alan'. 'Thank you so much for doing that', I said, 'and for everything really'.

BILLHEADS

above
Bailes' Celebrated
Pies and Sausages
came from Dawdon,
Sunderland.
The letter is dated
1945.

below right
An automobile for
Milburn & Co., Motor
Engineers in Whitby,
1929. Possibly a
stock block, it is also
die-stamped (raised
slightly)

opposite
A selection of
'billheads'. H. Field's
telegraphic address
would equally suit
Fremlins above

Design didn't really come into it with these letterheads. If you needed notepaper or invoices for your butchers business the chances are you would pass a handwritten note or scribble to your local printer. He (it was usually a bloke) would then set type in different sizes and fonts to a very regularised pattern. If you were, say, a pork butcher you could part with a couple more pounds and the printer would rummage amongst his stock blocks and find an engraved pig to snuffle about amongst the type. The result would be inked-up and a boy would come round with a proof.

The letterhead as we know it started out as a simple tradecard, but once business stationery got beyond swirling scripts, and advances were made with electro-stereotyping (ie: hard-wearing metal blocks made from line drawings) then your 'billhead' became a vital piece of publicity for your shop or company.

Printers and blockmakers began to incorporate a studio into their premises, and artists were set to engraving more pigs, sheep, trawlers, pork pies and, later, the latest model of car or cattle truck.

But by far the favourite gizmo, with the exception of medals won at obscure competitions, was the bird's eye view of your works. You didn't need to be a vast industry in order for a vast factory to stretch across your billhead, dwarfing people walking by and receding into a milky distance. Your customers would have been suitably assured of your competence, and, indeed, existence. Perhaps it was design after all.

HUNTS OF STUDLEY LIMITED

HORSE AND CATTLE TRANSPORTERS

STUDLEY WARWICKSHIRE

Memo. from
Ernest H. Harrison,
Butcher & Dealer.

Telegraphic Address:
CARBURINE HOLB LONDON.

Telephones:
7400.
7401.
MUSEUM 7402.
7403.
7404.
0550.

FBI · NATIONAL

RMT/ED

IN REPLY PLEASE QUOTE

"DECCO TURPS"
GLICO PETROLEUM, LIMITED
Alexandra House
ESTAB. 1888.
QUEEN SQUARE.
BLOOMSBURY.
LONDON, W.C.1. 9th May, 1927.

ALL QUOTATIONS SUBJECT TO REPLY BY RETURN OF POST UNLESS OTHERWISE STATED.

PLEASE ADDRESS ALL COMMUNICATIONS TO THE COMPANY.

RAMS:
MAIDSTONE

TELEP...
MAIDSTON...

FREMLINS LIMITED

TELEGRAMS:
"HOLLAND, LOSTOCK."

Lostock, Bolton, Feby 7th 1901

Mr E. H. Roberts Llandysilio

BOUGHT OF **W.H. HOLLAND & Co. LIMITED**

MANUFACTURERS OF

HOUSEHOLD TOILET and DRY SOAPS

FURNITURE CREAM
BAKING POWDER, LEMON CHEESE ETC.

Telepho...s:
HEAD ...ICE CENTRAL 5446.
CURING ESTABLISHMENT: CORPS 102.
PRIVATE: CORPS 1405.

Telegrams:
"JUMBO. HULL"

FROM **H. FIELD,**

STEAM TRAWLER OWNER
Herring & Haddock Curer.

Billingsgate,

HULL, July 3rd. 19

Telephones
MALTON 67
NORTON 176
DRIFFIELD 201

Bower's
of
56 WHEELGATE

BEEF & PORK
BUTCHERS
HAM & BACON
CURERS

MALTON

also at CHURCH STREET · NORTON
and MIDDLE ST. SOUTH · DRIFFIELD

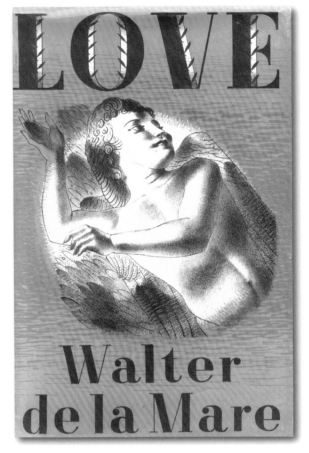

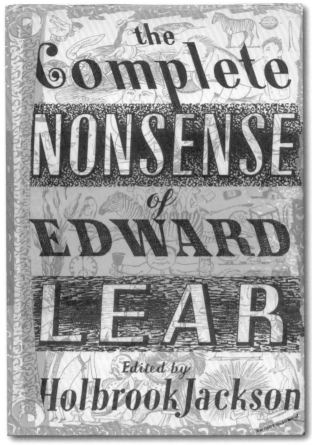

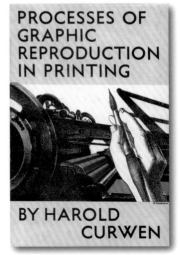

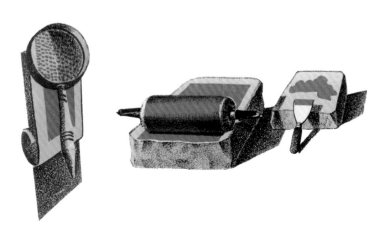

BARNETT FREEDMAN

In 1935 the GPO (General Post Office) produced a promotional film called *The King's Stamp* with music by Benjamin Britten. In it a small balding man with round rimless glasses is seen taking a brief from an official for the design of the stamps for King George V's Jubilee in the same year. 'Are there any restrictions?' the designer asks. 'No, only that the King's head should be on it, as before'. We then see the designer getting into a taxi and immediately starting to sketch out an idea. Back home he finishes a series of visuals, chooses one and sends it off by a GPO delivery boy who he looks out at anxiously from his upper window. The design is approved, 'Just thicken that 'N' up a bit', but what happens next is still a piece of magic to me, although it's only chemistry.

The designer goes to a platemaker where he draws his approved design, six times up from the final size, with a greasy pencil on a big thick piece of limestone. This is wetted and then inked, the image being the only part of the surface that accepts it. Proofs are taken off the stone, and these in turn are engraved for reproduction at Harrison's printers. Who print half-a-million stamps in an hour. The designer and GPO film star was Barnett Freedman, one of the most masterful artists who perfected the art of working on stone, or 'autolithography' as he called it. Even if his neat signature isn't there, his work is unmistakable, one of only a handful of artists who combined unique drawing skills with hand lettering.

BARNETT FREEDMAN *(continued)*

Barnett Freedman was born in 1901 to Jewish Russian immigrants in London's Stepney, and although much hampered by illness in his childhood he persevered through evening classes at St Martin's School of Art hoping to gain a London County Council scholarship. But his abilities were recognised by William Rothenstein at the Royal College of Art, and here he studied with Eric Ravilious and Edward Bawden, and along with Paul Nash, one of his tutors, all became friends. As did Paul's brother John. There's a lovely photograph of John Nash, Eric Ravilious and Barnett Freedman all in uniform as official War Artists, Freedman with a cigarette on, a habit he demonstrated throughout the GPO film.

His distinctive work and his proselytising about autolithography made him a favourite amongst both publishers like Faber and Faber and lithographic printers such as industry leaders The Baynard Press, Curwen Press and Chromoworks. There is a fabulous poster by him for Shell of an aeroplane flying low over lush countryside; an extraordinarily vibrant circus poster for the London Underground, and, something I'd missed entirely until recently, the logo for Ealing Film Studios. A timeless gift to the nation's culture, like Ravilious's two top-hatted cricketers that still adorn every copy of yellow-jacketed Wisden's. Barnett Freedman's fragile constitution finally overcame him, and he died, at work, in January 1958.

EX LIBRIS

To Plop with love
From "The Quins"
December 1943

BOOK Token

EXCHANGEABLE AT ANY BOOK TOKEN BOOKSHOP IN GT. BRITAIN & IRELAND
FOR A BOOK OR BOOKS OF THE HOLDER'S CHOICE TO THE VALUE SHOWN

the MOTHERLY and AUSPICIOUS

MAURICE COLLIS

The FABER Book of Children's VERSE

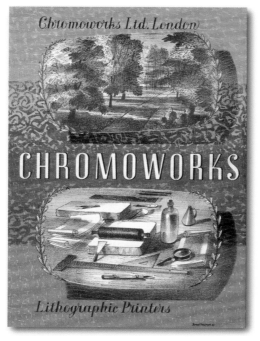

Chromoworks Ltd. London

CHROMOWORKS

Lithographic Printers

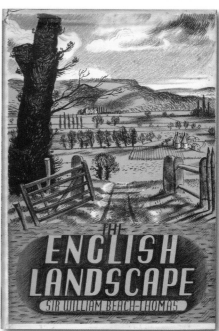

the ENGLISH LANDSCAPE

SIR WILLIAM BEACH-THOMAS

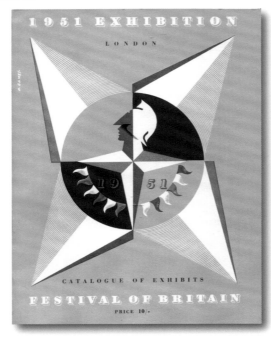

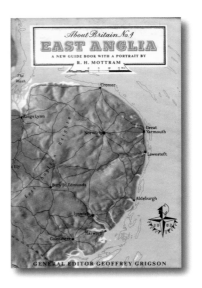

FESTIVAL OF BRITAIN

I was three years old when the 1951 Festival of Britain opened on its main site of what is now the South Bank in London. I knew nothing about it until a sticker bearing the Abram Games emblem suddenly adorned our cricket bat. The idea had started in 1947 for a centenary festival to commemorate the Great Exhibition of 1851, but after rejection by both a government committee and a useless Board of Trade, the Deputy Prime Minister took up the idea. He promoted it vigorously as 'a national festival that displayed the British contribution to civilisation, past, present and future, in the arts, science and industrial design'. In these years of grinding post-war austerity it also aspired to become 'A Tonic to The Nation'.

The main location was a bombed-out site between Waterloo Bridge and County Hall. Convenient for all transport links and with a River Thames frontage it was an inspired choice, one whose legacy has given us the South Bank and its range of cultural venues. Of all the buildings erected, only the Royal Festival Hall is still with us, but the souvenirs and memories of this national 'village fete' live on. The riverside walkway had a celebratory seaside promenade air, the modernist buildings gave a view of what a post-war Britain could look like. Displays both nostalgic and futuristic exercised professional designers, including a young Terence Conran before he discovered rustic French cookware.

above
Britannia cheekily turned into Mr Punch by Fougasse for the Festival issue of the eponymous magazine

above centre
Plaque for Bedfordshire village signs

above right
Postcard of a poster by Hans Unger

right
Geographia Festival Map

far right
Biro pen and stand, a Skylon souvenir

The South Bank Exhibition included the rotund Dome of Discovery, pavilions for The People of Britain and The Lion and The Unicorn (with a Country Life mural by Edward Bawden), cafés and restaurants with names like The Rocket, The Dairy Bar, The Regatta. A Dan Dare feature needled the London sky, an aluminium exclamation mark called the Skylon. Designed by Powell and Moya this futuristic pointer appeared to have no visible means of support. It found itself souvenir-ed as a Biro, just as Abram Games' Britannia-styled emblem turned up on everything from humble matchbooks to plastic paperweights, socks to horse brasses. And a cricket bat in Leicestershire.

above
Plastic paperweight
made by Wilmot
Breeden

right
*Pleasure Gardens
Guide* with cover
by Hans Tisdall

FESTIVAL OF BRITAIN *(continued)*

Upstream were the Pleasure Gardens in Battersea Park that perhaps recalled the days of 18th century Vauxhall and Ranelagh, with lanterns in the trees and music while you walked. The Far Tottering & Oyster Creek Railway, a three dimensional Emett cartoon, rattled around the arcades and pagodas, and of course there was all the fun of the fair with the Ghost Train, Flying Cars and a Sky Wheel that flung you 90 feet in the air. Special places for children included the News Chronicle Children's Zoo, Pets' Corner and Nestlé's Playland.

The Festival manifested itself outside of London, but I saw none of it. My older cousin went but had a row with his dad and came back almost straight away, so my first clue of what happened was probably watching the miraculous unfolding mechanisms of the Guinness Clock at Great Yarmouth, based on designers Lewitt-Him's extraordinary Battersea Park timepiece. And as I ate my McDonald's Penguin chocolate biscuit I little realised that its new wrapper was designed by Barnett Freedman and first shown at the Festival. Later I discovered the Festival village signs in Bedfordshire that had the emblem on a cast iron plate at one end, the county coat of arms at the other. Much later still I was given one of the spare Festival plates by the owner of the factory in Lowestoft that made them. A cause for more festivities.

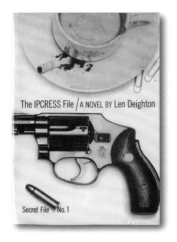
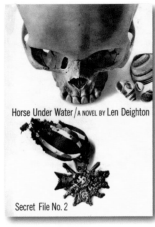

RAYMOND HAWKEY

above
The first four 'nameless hero' novels by Len Deighton

below
Penguin first editions. *Horse Under Water* sold out in 48 hours

opposite
Selection from the titles for *Oh! What a Lovely War* (1969)

It was one evening in a Leicester public library in 1964, and I was receiving books, dishing out fines and looking at the girl library assistants putting books back on the varnished shelves. 'Excuse me' said a voice behind me, startling me from my reverie. 'Have you any more by this chap?' A man in a pinstriped suit (who I later learnt was the local rep for Philips records) had just placed *The Ipcress File* on the counter top, and, as I picked it up and made for the shelves to see if we had any more Len Deightons, I just stared at the cover. So unusual for the time, it was a black and white photograph on a white background. A dirty cup had the legend 'War Office Canteen' on it, its saucer a stubbed out Gauloise, and, divided from it by a line of sparse type, the snout of a Smith & Wesson revolver poking its nose round on to the spine. On the back a rubber stamp had imprinted 'Downgraded to Unclassified'.

The inside flap of the dust jacket told me it was designed by Raymond Hawkey and running my finger along the 'D' shelf I came across *Horse Under Water* with a skull staring sightlessly at a be-barnacled Nazi medal. Next to it *Funeral in Berlin* with its hastily-packed leather bag showed not only the ubiquitous revolver but also a bottle of Milk of Magnesia tablets and, not quite hidden, a coyly-placed packet of Durex Gossamer. As the last of the sun shone through the tall windows of the library I realised something. I really did want to become a graphic designer.

AN ACCORD PRODUCTION

WENDY ALLNUTT
COLIN FARRELL
MALCOLM McFEE
JOHN RAE
CORIN REDGRAVE

MAURICE ROËVES
PAUL SHELLEY
KIM SMITH
ANGELA THORNE
MARY WIMBUSH

OH! WHAT A LOVELY WAR

And Guest Stars
DIRK BOGARDE
PHYLLIS CALVERT
JEAN PIERRE CASSEL
JOHN CLEMENTS
JOHN GIELGUD
JACK HAWKINS
KENNETH MORE

Casting
MIRIAM BRICKMAN
Location Manager
BRYAN COATES
Production Accountant
DEREK TARRANT
Production Secretary
ANN PATERSON
Construction Manager
ALBERT BLACKSHAW
Special Effects
RON BALLANGER
Property Buyer
RON BAKER
Stand-By Propertyman
JACK TOWNS
Electrical Supervisor
FRED ANDERSON

Editor
KEVIN CONNOR
Camera Operator
RONNIE TAYLOR

Directed by
RICHARD
ATTENBOROUGH

RAYMOND HAWKEY *(continued)*

above & centre
The 'In Transit Docket'
loosely inserted into
the first edition of
*An Expensive Place to
Die*. Photography by
Adrian Flowers

above right
The cover for *Bomber*,
using a detail from
J.M.W. Turner's painting
Fisherman at Sea
(1796)

Hawkey had met Deighton at the Royal College of Art, or when, as one story goes, party guest Hawkey was given the job of ejecting gatecrasher Deighton. After the latter had signed a contract for *The Ipcress File* in 1962, he asked Hawkey to design the jacket. 'Ray always came up with something original and striking, so I insisted on him doing the cover', remembers Deighton, 'It had no input from me'. The sales force at the publishers (at this stage Hodder & Stoughton) had a fit. But, as designer Mike Dempsey has said, this was 'one of the key moments in design history'. Hawkey went on to design innumerable Deighton covers, including that revolver again with a sprig of parsley in the barrel for *Action Cookbook*,

a very memorable one for Kingsley Amis's *The Anti-Death League,* and was responsible for putting two bullet holes actually punched out of the cover for the Pan edition of Ian Fleming's *Thunderball.* A superb high spot for me were the titles for the Deighton scripted film *Oh! What a Lovely War,* with Hawkey working as he always did with a brilliant photographer totally in tune with his vision, in this case David Cripps. (Others included Ken Denyer and Adrian Flowers.)

There is so much more. I particularly wanted to share with you the design he did for the *Bomber* poster, but my copy mysteriously caught fire. Hawkey would've appreciated that.

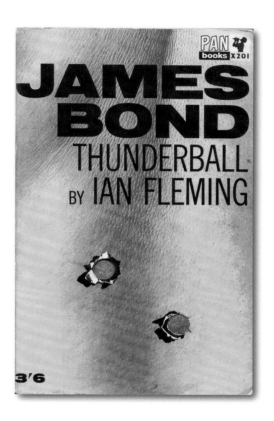

above
Perforated cover
for *Thunderball*

right
Publisher Gollancz
quibbled at the fee for
The Anti-Death League,
which was willingly paid
for by Kingsley Amis
himself, who quite
rightly thought it was
the best jacket he'd
seen thus far for his
work. Photography by
Adrian Flowers

THE FAMOUS AUTOMOBILE CARD GAME

TOURING

REG. U.S. PATENT OFFICE
IMPROVED EDITION
PARKER BROTHERS Inc. SALEM, MASS., NEW YORK, LONDON

FREMLINS
PLEASE CORK & RETURN THE CASK
ALE & STOUT
No 3
WHEN EMPTY
BITTERED ENTIRELY WITH HOPS

JOHN BULL
PRINTING
OUTFIT
MADE IN ENGLAND
No 12
"CARBAK" SERIES LONDON. S.E.5.
ENGLAND.

Y. KNOTT B.A.
REGULAR
DRINKER
OF
OXO

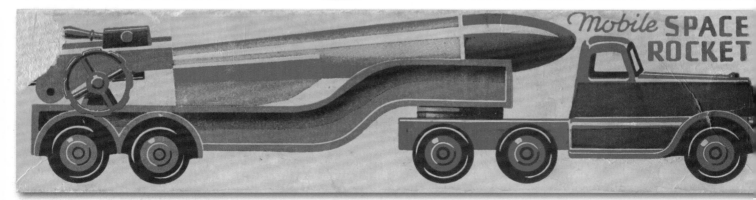

Mobile SPACE ROCKET

Ruddle's NUT BROWN ALE

Sparkling all bright beer
BREWED AT
LANGHAM BREWERY · OAKHAM RUTLAND

SMOKING MIXTURE

SWEET LEAF

DELIGHTFUL BLEND
OF THE MOST FRAGRANT
TOBACCOS.

THIS LABEL IS ISSUED BY THE IMPERIAL TOBACCO CO. (OF GREAT BRITAIN & IRELAND) LTD.

AN OPEN SECRET-

GOOD GOOD

MARMITE

MARMITE

DEFINITELY Does You GOOD

BACON BROTHERS CAMBRIDGE

ATHINA

Manufactured Solely by
BACON BROS
HAND MADE
CAMBRIDGE
NON SINE ANCHORA
CIGARETTES
MEDIUM

APPLE BRAND
SPARKLING CHAMPAGNE CIDER
REGISTERED
TRADE MARK
BOTTLED BY
ROBERT PORTER & Co LONDON

FOR DAILY WEAR BY EVERYMAN

THE LITESOME FOR MEN

REG?

NEXT TIME TRY THE
Mayfair Model

above
Pelican book cover
for *The Moscow
Puzzles*

above right
1973 *Design & Art
Direction Annual*

right
Royal Mail
weather stamps

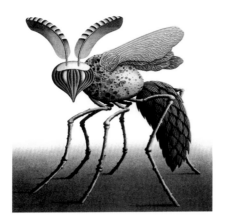
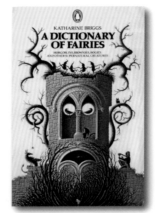
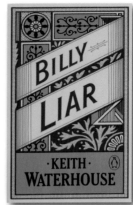

TONY MEEUWISSEN

There was a time in the 1970s and 80s when I was regularly going into bookshops in order to see if there were any recent Penguins or Pelicans. Not in search of literature or self-improvement but to see if the new covers were by either John Gorham (q.v.) or Tony Meeuwissen. I've never been one for tortuous conumdrums, Russian or otherwise, but Meeuwissen's artwork for *The Moscow Puzzles* sent me running to the till. As did his pastiche of a Woodbine cigarette packet, both front and back, for *Billy Liar*. It wasn't just the brilliant and witty ideas, it was the execution of the artwork. Meticulous to a dizzying degree, those of us who slaved over sheets of Kent artboard with our brushes and ruling pens knew just how much had gone into them. John Gorham once showed me the original for Tony's enigmatic cover for the 1973 *Design & Art Direction Annual*. The sheer craftsmanship was almost overwhelming in the detail of course, but it was the subject material that was so right.

Because it was a Meeuwissen view of the world. The monkey, the ships, the quayside capstan, they were all part of a unique place in which Tony knew that designers would go mad for that Old Salt matchbox. The fey illustration of the storm-shaken windmill with the cat (another favourite Meeuwissen *leitmotif*) immediately got snipped from the *Sunday Times Magazine* and pasted in my scrapbook, the accompanying article now long forgotten.

TONY MEEUWISSEN *(continued)*

Every morning the designer's gouache and watercolour gets prepared, and the intense concentration begins as it has done over the decades. Work that includes Royal Mail stamps (a Christmas one in 1984 won the Italian Francobollo d'Oro Award for the world's most beautiful stamp), books like *Remarkable Animals* and *The Witch's Hat,* (which also magically found its way into the ICI ad for duvets), and probably his most extraordinary achievement thus far which won him his second D&AD Gold Award in 1993. *The Key to The Kingdom* is a book, a set of playing cards and a saga of perseverance. Initiated by the V&A and supported by his agent Folio, cards and book just have to be seen to be believed.

The four of diamonds is a cat and a goldfish bowl, the six of diamonds is made from the red tiled roofs of a set of cottages. With milk bottles on one of the front steps. The nine of clubs is a set of paw prints leading from a spilt black ink bottle. With a cat on the label, of course. The Queen of Hearts is as subtle as she is beautiful.

Quite rightly Tony was made a Royal Designer for Industry (RDI) in 2013. Only 200 designers can hold this prestigious award at any given time. Do I have a favourite Meeuwissen? Well, I wish his insect on the cover of *The Penguin Dictionary of British Natural History* really existed. Provided it kept its distance of course.

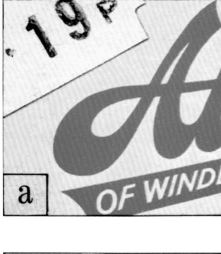

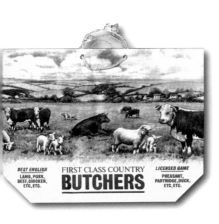

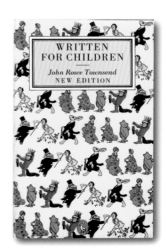

JOHN GORHAM

John was one of the most individual designers I ever met. And by individual I mean just that. You didn't go to him because he had a certain 'style', you used him because he was totally independent of any passing fad, he had outstanding creative ability that was resolved with staggeringly precise craftsmanship and on top of all that he was a genuinely decent bloke. You never knew what he would do next, but whenever I saw a superb piece of design in, say, the *Sunday Times Magazine*, the chances were that the tiny piece of type running up the side would say 'John Gorham'. An article on groceries needed a header for each of the alphabetical sections, and the result is a set of crops from brand labels. I asked John if he'd merely cut bits out of shopping and he looked astonished. 'It wouldn't work like that', he replied. 'I painted them all again so that they looked right'. Of course he did.

His name appears on countless Penguin and Pelican book covers, but even uncredited the work shone out. I remember picking up a letterhead in our office from Enigma, David Puttnam's film production company. At the top was a reproduction of Constable's 1821 *The Haywain*, and underneath a small line of carefully spaced type said 'Enigma'. Except the letter 'a' was upside down. Why's that? I thought, and then got it immediately. And knew it just had to be Mr. Gorham at work. (This is from memory. For once my itchy scissors missed snipping it out.) The cinema is perhaps where his work had most public exposure; the advertising for *Bugsy Malone*, the logo for *Revolution*, the letterhead for *Greystoke* and that so often copied script for *Fame*. Films and fame. Except the next week John could equally be reconstructing an old butcher's carrier bag for a magazine, or designing a letterhead for a mate.

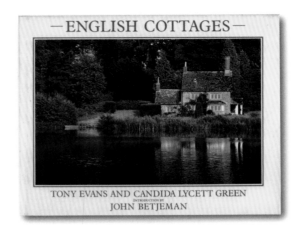

JOHN GORHAM (continued)

In 1974 John, with Paul Jennings, produced *The English Difference*. Again it was one of those books that I pounced on because the cover shouted at me across the shop. The entire book was a feast from start to finish, with contributions by writers of the calibre of W.G. Hoskins, George Ewart Evans and of course Jennings. It was illustrated by a gallery of artists that included David Gentleman, Michael Foreman, Harry Peccinotti and Peter Brookes. The cover was a superb collaboration with its painter, Tony Meeuwissen. Working with other artists was a great joy to John. Designing a set of decorated whisky tins for Glen Moray he discovered a company artist at the tin manufacturers who had exactly the finesse he was looking for, and one of the very best sets of Christmas stamps for the Royal Mail in 1990 were illustrated by Andrew Davidson.

The back cover of the Penguin edition of *The Onion Eaters* also credits a Bob Smithers. I'm not quite sure what Bob did; perhaps he ate the onions.

When Tony Evans photographed *English Cottages* (written by Candida Lycett Green) he insisted that John design the book. Publisher Weidenfeld & Nicolson weren't very keen to use an outside designer, but enlightened editor Mark Boxer insisted, and not only did the format (based on the proportions of a 35mm film frame) continue to be used on the rest of the long series that followed, it was also endlessly copied by other book designers. It seems so normal now, it wasn't then.

THE CRICKETERS

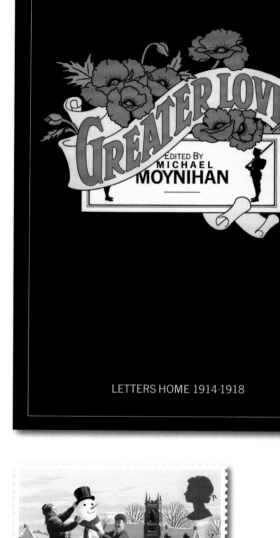

But for most of the time John ploughed a very singular furrow. A very English furrow, typified by his pub sign for The Cricketers, commissioned for Whitbread by John McConnell who at the time hadn't appreciated that John had played for Uxbridge. Which of course was the only game for this most English of Englishmen. The cover for *Greater Love* still stands to attention, a classic Gorham combination of type and hand-drawn lettering.

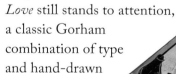

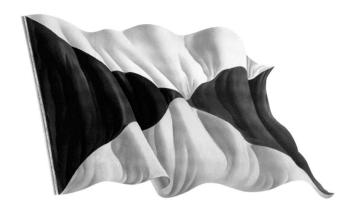

WOLFF OLINS *(1970s)*

above
Bovis logo and
hummingbird

above right
P&O Flag

right
Part of the Bowyers
identity

below
BOC (British Oxygen)
logo. The white
diagonal stripe ran
along the side of
tankers

It's a little difficult to imagine now just what an impact Wolff Olins made in the 1970s. Founded in London's Camden Town in 1965, Wally Olins wore big owl-like spectacles and was the business end, and Michael Wolff wore blue boiler-suits and designed like nobody else. By 1975 the company had grown and was esconced in an old butterscotch factory in Euston, giving the excuse for the walls and newly-installed ship's iron staircase to be painted yellow. That's when I arrived, staring agog at all that was going on around me. Michael was living upstairs and had a garden gate round the back with a Tony Meeuwissen painting on it, and Wally drove a Porsche. (Yellow, *naturellement*.)

They had recently re-designed the Carters Seed packets, probably the best a seed packet has ever been, and had remarkably persuaded Bovis, a heavyweight construction company, to adopt a lightweight orange hummingbird to flutter above their new logo. The original proposal was for a goldfish. Maritime P&O (originally Peninsular & Oriental) had their flag made to ripple in the breeze, and Bowyers of Wiltshire were given a pieman to sell their wares. Knowing the tendency for a Wolff Olins lunch to be vegetarian, they brought their own hams and pies to client meetings. I worked on an identity that involved at times huge green beavers (drawn by Harry Hargreaves) running on the sides of yellow lorries, and on my graduation was given a big book on the art of Walt Disney and an empty flip-top cigarette pack for my collection that had on it in black type: 'No thanks I'm trying to give them up'.

above

An original Carters
Seeds packet

right

An advertisement
from the *Practical
Householder* magazine
for April 1973 to
announce the new
Wolff Olins designed
packets

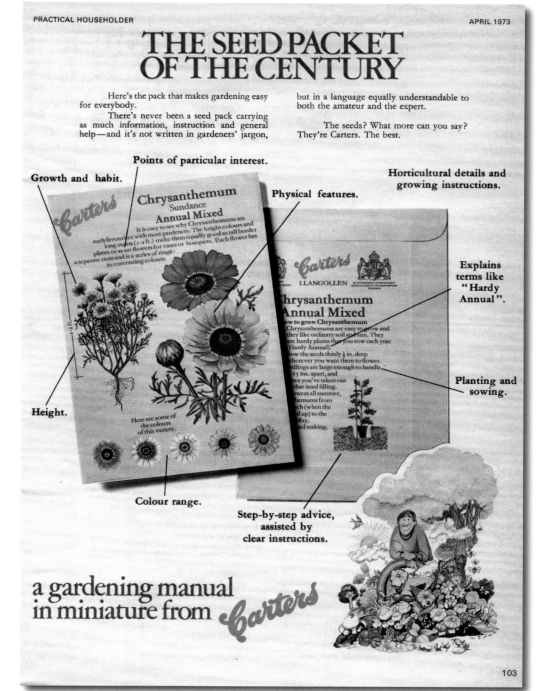

GALOSHES & PANAMAS

ENGLISH WEATHER

This is the weather the cuckoo likes,
And so do I;
When showers betumble the chestnut spikes,
And nestlings fly:
And the little brown nightingale bills his best,
And they sit outside at 'The Travellers' Rest',
And maids come forth sprig-muslin drest,
And citizens dream of the south and west,
And so do I.

This is the weather the shepherd shuns,
And so do I;
When beeches drip in browns and duns,
And thresh, and ply;
And hill-hid tides throb, throe on throe,
And meadow rivulets overflow,
And drops on gate-bars hang in a row,
And rooks in families homeward go,
And so do I.

'Weathers', Thomas Hardy

We probably don't go around in sprig-muslin much these days, but Hardy's beautifully evocative poem still has much resonance for us today. Two simple verses that neatly divide two kinds of weather we encounter.

No snow and ice here, no frost or fog. Just spring sunshine (one imagines also a blue sky and high clouds) and the rain leaving those droplets on the gate.

In England, wet or dry, the weather is the one topic of small talk that shouldn't cause offence. It's our common ground, the daily experience that forms the backdrop to everything we do, at least outdoors. Until I started taking photographs a little more seriously I hadn't taken much notice of climatic conditions; unless I'd ruined a car engine in a flood or not been able to get to the pub because of snow, or very occasionally fog. Living in London it hardly mattered, it was a case of whether I could get to the Underground station without getting soaked. Moving into very remote countryside it was all very different. What the weather was doing was always apparent, as immediate as the shrieks of animals meeting untimely ends in the woods that almost enclosed us. The trees lighting-up magnificently with autumn sunshine, thrashing about in winter gales and stooping heavily with snow.

RAIN

'We could do with some rain'. 'If only it would stop raining'. 'Never mind, it'll do the gardens good'. 'Did you hear the rain last night?' Personally I quite like a good downpour, but like everyone else I don't want it to ruin wedding days and I certainly don't want it when I've forgotten my umbrella. More than any other weather, rain fits our desire to have a good grumble. Forecasters always shake their heads and say things like 'More rain tomorrow *I'm afraid*', and then there's a drought and it's 'No sign of *any* rain yet'. A couple of weeks later it doesn't stop raining and poor folks get flooded out of their homes because someone's blocked a drainage channel. And I go about telling shop girls I'm building an Ark in my back garden and they're very welcome to book a cabin. No, we certainly need rain. We want puddles to jump in, we have to sing in it, we need raindrops on kittens.

I used to cycle to school, but when it rained I was given a lift in a mate's dad's car. First it was a dark green Ford Zodiac, but I did a rain dance when it was replaced by a Jaguar Mark 2. It made such a change from my dad cursing over the single wiper blade in his Popular, worked by a vacuum pipe from the engine which meant that the faster the car went the slower the blade struggled across the screen. I should hate rain, being forced to carry, and wear if necessary, a Pac-a-Mac plastic raincoat. I incurred Biblical wrath on holiday when I deliberately left it in a phone box in Robin Hood's Bay.

Blessed are the dead that the rain rains upon:
But here I pray that none whom once I loved
Is dying tonight or lying still awake
Solitary, listening to the rain…

'Rain', Edward Thomas (1916)

FOG

above
Prestley Hill above
Lyddington in
Rutland

below right
Fog warning signal,
The Lizard,
Cornwall

below
Princethorpe
College,
Warwickshire

An all-encompassing fog has the same attributes as a blanket covering of snow. The world changes; in fact as fog rolls in it can completely disappear. I probably wouldn't have wanted to have coughed my way through a London smog with men guiding buses by walking in front with blazing brands, but I do remember a fog in the 1950s that literally rolled down the street after my mum and I had been to the library and left us with about two yards of visibility. We waited for a bus that never came so we guided each other home by recognising lit shops and telephone boxes. But mostly by bumping into people, laughing and asking where we were. As day turned to night it also became quite frightening, but I recognised where we were by the pub at the bottom of our lane. Start of things to come perhaps.

Photographing lighthouses, I fell in with Alan Renton in Penzance who has written the definitive book (perhaps the only book) on fog horns. *Lost Sounds* tells of those giant stentorian horns that stood next to lighthouses and bellowed warnings of fog through trumpets that look like they would drop trousers for a five mile radius. Sounds we will probably never hear again except on rare and wonderfully evocative recordings, replaced now by high frequency emitters with no character whatsoever.

FROST

It was so cold in our house. But then in winter so was everybody else's it seemed, central heating being in the same class as holidays in France and cars with overdrive. Knowing no difference we just thought it was quite normal for Jack Frost to break in during the night and draw fern leaves on the *inside* of the north facing kitchen window. I still don't know how frost happens, but it's something to do with ice crystals forming in humid air in cold conditions, usually overnight. The idea of Jack Frost, the brittle featured myth of childhood, has of course now apparently been erased by one of those bug-eyed emetic characters in an animated film for the kiddies. Where is the magic of imagination, where is the thought that if your bedroom's cold enough your window might get drawn on?

Hoar frosts I relate to more now because the name comes from an Old English term meaning 'showing signs of old age', a frost that makes plants and trees look as if they've grown white hair. There is a particular joy in the depths of winter when out walking on the green lane near our village and seeing that the cow parsley stalks from the early summer are still making themselves noticeable with rimes of ice thickening their outlines. As they do for spiders' webs, or how they enhance the grain on a field fencing post. Entire trees covered in hoar frost appear so magical it's almost like a book illustration; you wouldn't be surprised to see the true Jack Frost hiding behind one of the icebound trunks.

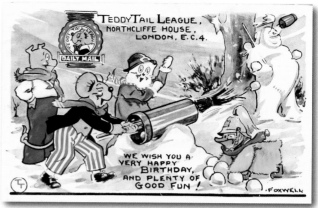

SNOW

I prayed for snow when I was small. And for the most part was disappointed. But then there would have been a morning when the light in my bedroom was somehow more cold and intense. Exceptional quietness outside, what slight noises there were muffled. My mother coming in, drawing back the curtains and saying 'Look outside'. And the world changed almost beyond recognition, purer, brighter. The fun of a hurried excitable breakfast and running out to join friends already in the lane, pressing ourselves against the hedge to let a skidding Humber pirouette by before we resumed piling snow down the backs of each other's gaberdine raincoats. Wellingtons to crunch to school in, joining others in the cloakroom standing in their melt-water, the headmaster ordering us not to snowball fight. But I'm afraid I did, so his finger beckoned me to join him in his office, the door closed and the cane swished down on my cold hand.

Everything slowed down, we huddled round stoves and teatime fires, overhearing grown-ups saying 'Wardley Hill's closed. Lorry drivers are stuck in their cabs' and I imagined all those Albions and Seddons and men under rugs with tartan-patterned Thermos flasks. The lamplighter was early, cursing even more than usual, as I went out with my Pifco torch to find animal tracks. No badger's or fox's, just next door's dog and our cat. Sometimes the snow stayed around for days, but more often it was a one day wonder, quickly turning to grey slush, the drains cascading with rushing water. Until the next time.

WIND

above
Force 5 on the
Beaufort Scale, drawn
by Robert Ayton for
*The Ladybird Book of
The Weather* 1962

top
A wind-bent silver
birch at Sandscale
in Cumbria

'Scattered to the four winds' we say, meaning to the four corners of the earth as the cardinal directions dictate on our weather vanes: north, south, east and west. In Greek mythology they had names: Boreas from the north, Notus from the south, Eurus the east and probably the most well known, Zephyrus from the west, our prevailing wind. The wind coming from the west blows the detritus of a city eastwards, which they say is the reason why in the past the east end of cities were much more disadvantaged than the west. West End, East End, but whilst some knob in Belgravia might agree I wouldn't want to have the discussion with anybody from Hackney.

I quite like wind, and was always fascinated by the illustrations in my *Ladybird Book of The Weather* explaining the Beaufort Scale. From Force 0 with the smoke from factory chimneys going straight up, through a limp slightly stirring flag on a church tower, Force 2, to a Force 10 where I was alarmed by the picture of a chimney collapsing. In October 1987 I was living 20 miles away from the epicentre of the Great Storm near Sevenoaks and I ended up in the foetal position on the landing thinking an atom bomb had gone off. What seemed like an attack of grapeshot was the pebbledash coming off the house and showering across the windows. Up to 15 million trees were lost that night.

At the other end of the scale a summer breeze can be just about perfect. In his book *Nature Near London*, Richard Jefferies stood on Beachy Head in Sussex and recounted: 'It is air without admixture. It comes from the south, the waves refine it; if inland, the wheat and flowers and grass distil it. The great headland and the whole rib of the promontory is wind-swept and washed with air; the billows of the atmosphere roll over it.' I still like it when it's difficult to stand up, providing it doesn't do the classic trick of turning my umbrella inside out. But out in any wind a friend says she always feels like she's being assaulted. 'All that unpredictability and buffeting, I don't like it'.

For me it is just so elemental, an invisible force hoovering across the landscape. And the way it can slowly creep up on you: weather vanes creaking with change, just as windmill sails and oast house cowls once did; my chimney coming to life with an increasingly loud moan, a distant unlatched door starting to bang.

SUN

above
The rewards for waiting. December light at Kirby Hall, Northamptonshire

below left
A celebratory sun for gimp pins

below right
Ploughing at sunrise. Or sunset. Young Farmers Club badge, c1950

George Formby's song 'Turned Out Nice Again' became his catchphrase, although he didn't sing it in the 1941 film of the same name. It's a phrase we use all the time in England, sometimes even when it's bucketing down with rain, but generally we say it in appreciation of the sun finally coming out again. If you're a photographer who works outdoors, lighting from the sun is crucial. Not that you need glaring sunlight all the time, the best pictures get taken when there's some cloud around to give contrast to a hemisphere of blue, and a low sun is good because it acts like a side-on spotlight.

Shots of buildings benefit from having shadows helping to bring out details, so very often much of my time can be spent waiting for the sun. And giving up and driving away so that ten minutes later it suddenly comes out in an uninterrupted burst. Filming will often take place in what cinematographers call 'The Golden Hour' which is non-specific to a particular time, but is nearly always in late afternoon or early evening sunlight. Film-makers still can't rely on perfect sunshine when they want it, and for location interiors lights with big diffusers are placed up against the windows to great effect.

above left
Sunset over the lost village of Othorpe, Leicestershire

above right
Near Blaston, Leicestershire, after the storm

below left
Cover image from *The English Sunrise*

below right
Sun Brand Safety Matches

The drama of sunlight will of course usually happen at sunset, when atmospheric conditions will often give us spectacular western horizons. They can't be planned for, and the best are always impromptu. Sunrises with a sun can be good, their dramatic appearances has led us to use them as a *leitmotif* for optimism. Photographer Tony Evans and Brian Rice produced a collection in their book *The English Sunrise*, including garden gates, doormats, shopfronts, cinemas and even the leather door panel of an SS1 Jaguar saloon. Albion lorries had one as a badge above their radiator grilles.

Sunshine doesn't necessarily mean heat, as England knows all too well. Most of us want it to be a scorcher for our barbeques but don't want it to melt our ice creams, we want to encourage a tan perhaps, but don't want to be spit roasted. Since around 1980 we've averaged about 1,500 hours of sunlight a year, with places like Eastbourne on the south coast getting the most and Penrith in the frozen north the least. Just having the sun out is a great benefit, but I do like a good thunderstorm after a particularly humid day. Preferably one that doesn't wake me up in the middle of the night.

BOOTS & BONNETS

CHARACTERFUL CARS

above

An Automobile
Association badge
from the era of
saluting patrols
and yellow
handbooks

opposite

1951-1959 tax
discs for MLU 943,
a black Austin.
A little paper trail
for a car probably
bought in London
but kept in West
Sussex for at
least nine years.
No more will we
have the pleasure
of sitting outside
post offices
tearing around
the perforations

It wasn't until I was a teenager that my father bought a car. Until then the cars I was most familiar with were those in close promity to the house: A 1920's dark blue Morris Oxford next door that rushed me to hospital to have stitches in my head; a black Morris 10 three doors away belonging to my friends' dad that we all sat in making car noises and the occasional visitor to our garage that I was forbidden to go in but did. Up the lane was a black Humber Hawk, down the lane was a pre-war SS Jaguar. In black. I didn't go trainspotting, I stood outside the pub on the main road with my *Observer's Book of Automobiles* (the 1957 edition) and stared at the traffic. So I learnt about Austin Cambridges and Westminsters, Ford Consuls, Zephyrs and Zodiacs, Hillman Minxes, Singer Hunters. And the odd exotic foreigner: the incomparable Citroën DS19, a stray DeSoto Fireflite from the nearby American airbase; and very occasionally the Mercedes 300SL Gullwing belonging to a local builder. On Sundays we might get a lift back home from church in a Ford Prefect or a Lanchester 14. Both in black.

Even though they could drip oil, be somewhat unpredictable to steer and had engines that periodically need 'de-coking', motor cars once had character in boot loads. They all looked as though a draughtsman had sucked a pencil over a drawing board or a stylist had stepped back after taking shavings off a wooden maquette. I'm hoping car designers today start out with a scribble somewhere, if not on the back of a fag packet then across a serviette in a lunchtime brasserie, but still something is missing. Before designers got going cars could look very similar, then, they didn't. So why is it that cars now look much the same as each other again? An Audi morphing into a BMW that wants to be an an XJ Jaguar. I expect it's to do with 'market forces' (ie China) or 'dovetailing into the customer's expectations' or some such eyewash. Just as BP make out their initials stand for 'Beyond Petroleum', I'm sure the focus groups talk of 'extending the proposition': you like the Fiat 500? Maybe you'd like the Fiat 500 kettle. Anyway, here are a small handful of cars of character that have at some time made my pulse quicken.

ALVIS 12/50

'…the typical Alvis of the Vintage period remains the 12/50; we cannot but consider it one of the classic designs of the time, and remains of all Vintage sports cars the one which needs least apology'. So wrote Clutton and Stanford in *The Vintage Motor Car,* and I can vouch for the veracity of this as I'm very familiar with the example here. To be driven not only exceptionally well but at speed by its current owner down sunlit Northamptonshire lanes is both exhilarating and heart-stopping in equal measure. The 1496cc engined HP 8835, capable of 70 mph, was registered in Coventry in August 1924 and cost £615. The body was made by another firm, Cross & Ellis. At this time car manufacturers tended to stick to what they knew, producing all the mechanicals on to which a completed body could be lowered. This practice is probably most well-known with Rolls-Royce car engineering once having coachbuilt bodies dropped on them by the likes of Mulliner.

Perhaps you remember Ken Russell's *Elgar,* a BBC Monitor film of 1962. Many unforgettable images come to mind: young Elgar on a pony, adult Elgar sliding down a field on a tea tray and towards the end an elderly Elgar in a motor car climbing up a track in the Malvern Hills in Worcestershire. With his dogs sticking their snouts out into the wind. This is the actual car, filmed after the owner, the Hon. Jim Wallace (the current Lord Dudley) had fully restored it, including putting the Alvis into this blue paintwork. Cue the *Introduction & Allegro for Strings.*

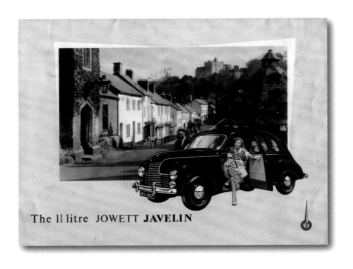

The 1¼ litre JOWETT **JAVELIN**

JOWETT JAVELIN

On our meandering way to school we always looked out for the steeply banked driveway that was home to a Jowett Javelin. After all the post-war, and indeed pre-war, cars around in the mid-fifties this was something that at least tried to look futuristic. The sloping back that seemed to invite sliding down, and the vaguely contemporary Detroit radiator grille, were all design notes we subconsciously absorbed. Unreliably I'd always thought this example was in that dusty pale green beloved by utility companies, but I now see it must have been a *saloon de luxe* in 'metallic grey'. It would also have had a walnut-grained dashboard, hide upholstery, a detachable picnic tray and possibly an HMV Radiomobile car radio as an extra.

Jowett Brothers Ben and William started the company as a cycle business in the Bradford of 1901, producing their first car in 1906. By 1922 they had such a following that an owners' club was inaugurated, becoming the earliest of such things for a single marque. Jowett's went on to also make Bradford vans, and towards the end of their time the Jupiter sports car. The Javelin was designed by Gerald Palmer during the war, and production lasted from 1947 to 1953. 23,307 Javelins were made before Jowett's finished production in 1954 and were bought by tractor manufacturers International Harvester. Kindly abortionist *Vera Drake* drove a Jowett Javelin in the eponymous film by Mike Leigh (2004).

Austin Healey 3000

Jaguar 3.4 Litre

Morgan Spare Wheel & Filler Cap

Austin Seven

Land Rover Series 1

Vauxhall Wyvern

rd Zephyr

Rover 2200

Iman RAF Staff Car

Frazer Nash Filler Cap

ntley Badge

MGB Radiator Grille

RILEY RM 1½ LITRE

Riley RMs were the last cars to be produced independently by the company before the merger of the Nuffield Organisation with Austin to form the British Motor Corporation (BMC) in 1952. First produced in 1945, these superb looking cars with their fabric-covered roofs, faired-in headlamps and duotone colour schemes were much sought after by drivers who had to accommodate the family but still fancied something a bit 'sporty'. There was a 2½ litre version (you can tell them initially by their pale blue badges) and a stunning convertible roadster made chiefly for the American market. At first they were made in Coventry, the car capital of England, but production moved to the MG works in Abingdon in 1949.

I bought a black 1956 example in 1972 (below), quickly realising that my lack of mechanical knowledge might be a drawback. Yet in spite of curious knockings and ill-defined grindings coming from the engine, it never failed to complete a journey in the couple of years or so I drove it at full-bore around England. Usually the engine was as sweet as a sewing machine, (with a not dissimilar sound), the gears were selected by a short little lever and if it failed to turn over on a cold morning there was always the starting handle. The seats were comforting leather, the dashboard wooden and the contemporary car radio warmed-up with humming valves. (I fully expected Frankie Laine to come on halfway through *Mule Train*.)

MORRIS OXFORD TRAVELLER

above
The 1957 sales
brochure cover

below
An earlier Morris
badge with a
pictogram of an
'ox' and a 'ford',
denoting the city of
their manufacture

opposite top
All Steel details.
Note the
semaphore-style
indicator on the left

opposite
50 cubic feet of
luggage space with
the rear seat
folded down

Strictly speaking, this is the Morris Oxford
All Steel Traveller, Series IV, made from
1957-60. I found this rare example in a car
show at Thoresby Hall in Nottinghamshire,
and was so taken with it I went in search of
the sales brochure. On receipt I found that
the object of my desire was finished in Dark
Green and Island Green and the sales blurb
told me: 'This new Oxford All-Steel Traveller
is not only robust, colourful, and handsome,
but also has line and design to make it the
most accommodating and versatile multi-
purpose car ever.' Previously the Oxford
Travellers were a larger version of the Morris
Minor 'woody' with an ash frame, but there
was something about this less overtly
rustic version that captured my
imagination.

I wrote at the time, still excited by my
discovery, that I saw it 'drawn up outside
a Southern Region railway station on the
Sussex Kent borders. Early evening light
reflecting off the chrome as the signal arm
elevates to welcome the 5.15 from Victoria, a
red setter getting excited in the back as a lady
in a pink gingham blouse drums red painted
nails against the steering wheel'. Back up at
a tile-hung house behind rhododendrons
in the Weald it would make an ideal garage
companion to an indigo blue Mark IX Jaguar
or even a burgundy Bristol 406. Coming back
down to earth it must have been ideal for the
two nurserymen to let the back seat down for
their boxes of flowers and still have room
in the front for a dog to mist up
the windscreen.

JAGUAR XK120

There was probably only one XK120 in the world that was bought brand new and kept by its owner until he died. And that was the Old English White (or 'cream' as the log book had it) two-seater roadster belonging to motoring correspondent and politician Alan Clark. Bought in November 1950 from City Motors in Oxford whilst still an undergraduate, he later lived in Monte Carlo where yawning gendarmes may have caught a glimpse of him in the early hours swinging it around the streets with three, sometimes four, ballet dancers squeezed in with him.

The XK120 has always had a slightly raffish appeal; its appearance in 1950s films was an ideal accompaniment to Leslie Phillip's-style blandishments, or as a prop for Jayne Mansfield to sinuously drape herself over. And it still happens now. Julian Temple used one in his deeply impressive *London: The Modern Babylon* (2012) for a Soho habitué

to reminisce in, and the red example shown above recently had a brief drive-on part parked on King's Parade Cambridge in the first episode of *Grantchester* (2014).

This red roadster is about to be scrubbed up for new adventures, the dreamlike Fixed-Head Coupé is almost finished after a major restoration. Either way, an XK120 is ideal for English excursions. Just fill up your Fortnum & Mason hamper, then unpack it all because it won't fit in the boot, and finally take to the road with a suitable and like-minded companion to further explore the highways and byways of Unmitigated England.

BOOKS

above

The longhand fuel
for book writing:
The Swan Ink
'Last Drop' Bottle

Norfolk: A Shell Guide *Wilhelmine Harrod* (Faber & Faber 1982)

Poppy-Land *Clement Scott* (re-published by Christine Stockwell 1992)

Romney Marsh *John Piper* (Penguin 1950)

Joanna Godden *Sheila Kaye-Smith* (Penguin 1951)

Cross Country *Peter Ashley* (John Wiley 2011)

The Moving Metropolis *edited by Sheila Taylor* (Lawrence King 2001)

Underground Architecture *David Lawrence* (Capital Transport 1994)

Howards End *E.M. Forster* (Penguin 1960)

Underground Art *Oliver Green* (Studio Vista 1990)

How Household Names Began *Maurice Baren* (Michael O'Mara books 1997)

Murray's Berkshire Architectural Guide *Edited by John Betjeman & John Piper* (John Murray 1949)

Flora Britannica *Richard Mabey* (Sinclair-Stevenson 1996)

Poisonous Fungi *John Ramsbottom* (Penguin 1945)

Edible Fungi *John Ramsbottom* (Penguin 1948)

Vanishing Victoriana *Lucinda Lambton* (Elsevier Phaidon 1976)

Messenger & Co. Ltd. Horticultural Section Catalogue (c1920s)

Eric De Maré *Robert Elwall* (RIBA 2000)

An English Eye: The Photographs of James Ravilious *Peter Hamilton* (The Bardwell Press 2007)

Somerset *Maxwell Fraser* (Great Western Railway 1934)

Orlando A Seaside Holiday *Kathleen Hale* (Country Life 1952)

Graphic Design: Visual Comparisons *Alan Fletcher, Colin Forbes, Bob Gill* (Studio Books 1963)

A Tonic to The Nation *Edited by Mary Banham & Bevis Hillier* (Thames & Hudson 1976)

The Key to the Kingdom *Tony Meeuwissen* (Pavilion 1992)

The Ladybird Book of The Weather *F.E. Newing & Richard Bowood* (Wills & Hepworth 1952)

Lost Sounds *Alan Renton* (Whittles Publishing 2001)

The English Sunrise *Brian Rice & Tony Evans* (Mathews Miller Dunbar 1972)

The Vintage Motor Car *Cecil Clutton & John Stanford* (Batsford 1954)

Backfire *Alan Clark* (Weidenfeld & Nicolson 2001)

APPENDIX

Naves & Chancels

Finding ruined Norfolk churches is challenging but great fun. Study the Ordnance Survey maps first, with Landrangers 132 & 133 as a good start. Look out for the gothicky script that says 'Church (rems of)' and then put your map-reading skills to the test. Remember, some will be almost impossible to find, hidden away in woods and away from a decent road, and others will now be on private property. Many churches are of course remote but not ruined. In these cases you'll need to find the keeper of the key. If you're really lucky there will be a phone number pinned-up in the porch. The churches on the Romney Marsh are much easier to find, and are almost always open. Although East Guldeford has never been open on my visits and I've never had the time to find the key, sadly. These sites for church trusts are very useful:

Norfolk Churches Trust

www.norfolkchurchestrust.org.uk

The Churches Conservation Trust

www.visitchurches.org.uk

The Romney Marsh Historic Churches Trust

www.romneychurches.net

Bus Stops & Escalators

This is easy, a one-stop job. Almost. The London Transport Museum in Covent Garden is a must, even if you haven't the remotest interest in tube stock or the varieties of RF single deckers, you will find much to fascinate. How travel used to be on horse-drawn buses, trams, trolley buses, trains. The maps we used, the posters we looked at. The shop, as I have said, is a dangerous place. I defy anyone not to find something desirable. If you subscribe to the website you'll also get to know when the LT Museum Depot in Acton has an open weekend. *www.ltmuseum.co.uk*

Tea & Clockwork

The first port of call for Unmitigated brands must be Robert Opie's Museum of Brands, Packaging & Advertising. I could stay in here all day until ushered gently out at closing time. Every now and then it seems that Robert's incredible museum has to be packaged-up itself and moved, but by the time you're reading this it should be safely home at 111-117 Lancaster Road, London W11 1QT. *www.museumofbrands.com.* Tiptree: It's well worth a visit to this area anyway, particularly down at Tollesbury with much maritime goings-on, a lightship and yacht stores. And then back up the road to Wilkins' jam factory. Find out about the tea rooms and factory tours at: *www.tiptree. com.* For Hornby clockwork trains you can wind yourself up at the Brighton Toy & Model Museum on your visit to the south coast resort. Appropriately they're underneath Brighton station.

www.brightontoymuseum.co.uk

Cakes & Ale

You will get a great view of Abingdon from the roof of that stunning County Hall, and the Thames-side area is very redolent of *Three Men in a Boat* (Jerome K. Jerome reckoned they brewed a bitter ale in what was left of the abbey). *www.english-heritage.org.uk/visit/places/abingdon.* If you don't fancy trolling down the M2 to Faversham you can now take a very fast train from St Pancras International. Even stopping everywhere it still only takes an hour. If you take the train you can allow yourself a decent intake of Shepherd Neame, even within a few steps of the brewery: *www.shepherdneame.co.uk.* Break the long haul up to Cromer in Fakenham, and make it a Thursday for the market.*www.fakenham.info.* Tuesday is market day in Melton Mowbray. Get here early for the bucolic pleasures of the cattle market, and keep room for a Grasmere Farms breakfast. *www.meltonmowbraymarket.com*

Daffodils & Monsters

There are of course any number of books on the nature of England. At the top end I can thoroughly recommend the volumes being published in the British Wildlife Collection. So far there are: *Mushrooms* by Peter Marren; *Meadows* by George Peterken and *Rivers* by Nigel Holmes & Paul Raven. All have fabulous covers by Carry Akroyd. Everybody should have these four Ladybird books by E.L. Grant Watson: *What to Look for in Spring, Summer, Autumn & Winter,* each beautifully illustrated by Charles Tunnicliffe RA, and after over half a century still so useful.

Black & White

Film cameras are becoming very sought after again, so naturally they need to be fed with film. But hurry, hurry. You can still buy 35mm films like Kodak's Tri-X and T-Max (not to be confused with the bargain clothes shop) and good old Ilford's HP5. However, just as music is back on vinyl again, I'm sure film will return. Of course it's always interesting to scroll down the options in your digital camera. Exhibitions of the two photographers I mention are rare, but do take a look at: *www.jamesravilious.com*

Lobsters & Lilos

Watch the original 1947 *Brighton Rock* film directed by John Boulting for the full-on flavour of a town only an hour from London. (The more recent film relies heavily on Eastbourne.) Frequent trains run to Weston-super-Mare from Bristol, otherwise it's junction 21 on the M5. The very rural railway line from Saxmundham to Aldeburgh is closed, except for a stretch going into Sizewell power station to pick up nuclear waste. So it's off the A12 Ipswich to Lowestoft road and then down the A1094. Take M.R. James' ghost story *A Warning to The Curious & Other Ghost Stories* to read. Essential reading for Cornwall is the Shell County Guide by John Betjeman and his very evocative Cornish poems. And immerse yourself in everything to do with the Rev. Hawker of Morwenstow. My best thing to do in Blackpool? Take a tram (preferably a vintage 'balloon') from Starr Gate, in the south, eleven miles up the seafront to Fleetwood.

Pipes & Pencils

See what it's like to mix some Winsor & Newton's Designers Gouache with water and just play around with it on a sheet of good watercolour paper. Two books by the master designer Alan Fletcher are a joy to immerse oneself in: *Beware of Wet Paint* and the doorstop *The Art of Looking Sideways*. The Festival of Britain is comprehensively explained in *A Tonic to The Nation* listed here in Books. There really ought be a proper monograph on John Gorham (I have tried) but we do have Tony Meeuwissen's *The Key to The Kingdom*, as good for playing cards with as it is for reading.

Galoshes & Panamas

Just get out and enjoy it, whatever the weather. If you get caught in a storm hurry back home and whilst your clothes dry by the fire you can read *British Weather Disasters* by Ingrid Holford with relief.

Boots & Bonnets

Two major collections of characterful cars ought to be seen, at the National Motor Museum in Hampshire and the Heritage Motor Centre in Warwickshire:

www.beaulieu.co.uk

www.heritage-motor-centre.co.uk

But always look out for local car rallies, and fabulous vehicles of all types can be seen at the Great Dorset Steam Fair and the Wrotham Steam Rally on Wrotham Hill in Kent:

www.gdsf.co.uk

www.wrotham.org

Ways to see Unmitigated England
Walking: this way you see more (far left). By slow train or bicycle: no Lycra, Pashley Classic 33 or Guv'nor preferred (centre). Pack up a 1959 Hillman Husky with hampers of pork pies and cordials, maps and dogs. Family members if there's still room (above).

THANKS

Many thanks to Clive Aslet for his Preface

Stephen Allen, George Ashley, Kathy Ashley, Lucy Ashley, Wilf Ashley, Bassetts Liquorice Allsorts, Blists Hill Victorian Town, David Campbell, Barbara Campey, Christopher Clarke, Teresa Cox, English Heritage, Pauline Gorham, Richard & Jane Gregory, Tom Harris, Mary Hawkey, Stean Jackson, Stuart Kendall, Geoff Laurens, Loose Cannon Brewery Abingdon, Tony Meeuwissen, Edward Milward-Oliver, The National Trust, Biff Raven-Hill, Lily Sampson, Margaret Shepherd, The Shuttleworth Collection, Ken & Hazel Wallace, Chris Wild, Tyler Bennett at Wilkin & Sons, Philip Wilkinson, Nick Wright

Images

Most of the images in this book are from the author's personal collections. Others have come from various sources; the author and publisher would like to credit: Page 9 Autochrome Image © CORBIS; Pages 40-41 Ellis Posters & Page 134 Green Line Poster © TfL from the London Transport Collection; Pages 54-55 Train image in co-operation with Stean Jackson; Pages 98-99 © Joyce Raven-Hill; Pages 102-103 Eric De Maré / RIBA Collections; Pages 106-107 James Ravilious © CORBIS; Page 141 An Accord Production for Paramount Pictures 1969; Page 154 Flag courtesy of P&O Heritage Collection; Page 171 Hare Mascot © Nick Wright; Page 180 Jaguar XK120 Badge © Tom Harris

Text

For permission to reprint copyright material the author and publisher gratefully acknowledge the following:

p.21 Reproduced with permission of Ian Fleming Publications Ltd, London GOLDFINGER Copyright © Ian Fleming Publications Ltd 1959 www.ianfleming.com

p.24 Extract from *Joanna Godden* by Sheila Kaye-Smith, Penguin, 1921 © The Estate of Sheila Kaye-Smith 1921. Reproduced by kind permission of Peters Fraser & Dunlop (www.petersfraserdunlop.com) on behalf of The Estate of Sheila Kaye-Smith.

p.38 Extract from *Howards End* by E.M. Forster. Reproduced by kind permission of The Provost and Scholars of King's College, Cambridge and The Society of Authors as the E.M. Forster Estate.

p.60 Extract from *Murray's Berkshire Architectural Guide* by John Betjeman and John Piper, John Murray, 1949. © The Estate of John Betjeman and © The Estate of John Piper. Reproduced by kind permission of John Murray Press, an imprint of Hodder & Stoughton.

p.80 Extract from *Pravda* by Howard Brenton and David Hare © Howard Brenton and David Hare, 1985. Reproduced by kind permission of Bloomsbury Methuen Drama, an imprint of Bloomsbury Publishing Plc.

p.90 Extract from 'MCMXIV' by Philip Larkin. © The Estate of Philip Larkin, 1964. Reproduced by kind permission of Faber & Faber Ltd.

p.107 Extract from Alan Bennett's Introduction to *An English Eye* by Peter Hamilton, Bardwell Press, 2007. © Alan Bennett, 2007. Reproduced by kind permission of Alan Bennett.

p.174 Extract from *The Vintage Motor Car*. © Clutton, Cecil and John Stanford. The Vintage Motor Car (1954). Reproduced with kind permission of B.T. Batsford, part of Pavilion Books Company Limited.

Every reasonable effort has been made to contact copyright holders of material reproduced in this book. Any omissions are entirely unintentional and should be notified to the publisher, who would be glad to hear from them and will ensure corrections are included in any reprints.

above

A Northampton florist's emblem, c1930

opposite

Britains farm signpost

INDEX

Figures in **bold** refer to illustrations

The Author wearing his King's College Cambridge
rowing cap. He didn't go to King's and certainly
never rowed for them. Records in Wisden of his
cricketing career seem equally lightweight.